White Washed Woke

by
Gary Wolfe

Table of Contents

INTRODUCTION

I've had many trepidations about writing this book. I was worried about what people would think and how my words would be taken. But after looking at the state of the world and society, the state of my people and the conversations I've had with my people, I have to say something.

I wasn't quite sure how to approach it at first. I thought I should write as the reader, learning as we go along, but I can't unlearn the things I've learned, unlive the experiences I've had and unread the books I've read. So, I decided to write it in the style of who it's for: my people. My FBAs (Foundational Black Americans), African Americans, ADOSs (American Descendants of Slavery), Indigenous, Negroes, Blacks, Niggas, and all melanated people out there in the world. What I'm going to say won't be accepted by my people at first. In fact, it'll probably make some of y'all downright mad. I hope that in time you'll understand what I say is not to hurt or diminish. It will be the truth, my truth, and our truth. I love us. And I don't want to lie to my people because we've been lied to for way too long.

So, what's this book about? It's about waking up and coming to the realization of how the world perceives you as a Black person in today's society and throughout history. Whether you're sleep, woke, aware or conscious, my goal with this book is to help ease the transition through each phase. Most importantly, I want to help guide those who have just woken up and feel they have no one to turn to. I want you all to know that you are not alone in your thoughts, emotions, and rage. Like James Baldwin said, "To be negro in this country and relatively conscious is to be in a state of rage almost all of the time." But now it's not just America, it's the world. I'm going to touch on a few subjects that may make people uncomfortable (i.e., segregation, law enforcement, history, mixed relationships, slavery, religion, trauma), but uncomfortable conversations are where personal growth happens. Like Gil Scott-Heron said, "The revolution will not be televised" meaning, there must be a revolution of the mind first.

Most of what I'm saying is not new and the

final message will not be new either, but sometimes the messenger makes a difference in how the message is received and whether it resonates with future generations. And I, as the messenger, have been on the other side. It may look greener, but it is only an imitation of the original (which we'll come to later).

Now, I am aware that other nationalities might pick up this book. But please know this conversation is for my people. You are more than welcome to "listen." At any time if you don't like the direction it's heading, I won't be insulted if you decide not to continue reading. All I ask for is your honesty when asked why you decided not to continue.

I'll also be using the word "nigga" in this book. I know some of you will see this and say, "This dude claims to be conscious but he says 'nigga'." Here's the deal with that: I've observed as other cultures have infiltrated us. Our jobs, social circles, neighborhoods, entertainment, style, music, families, and cookouts. Although they infiltrate, they all know, if you ain't Black and you call a Black person a nigga, that's grounds for a beatdown. It's the only thing we still have (taken from the word 'Negus'), and until we are given something tangible, I'm gonna say it.

Now, if you're still reading, I'm going to ask you a question, my brothers and sisters. This question will determine if this book is for you. I've asked people this question and most of the time I can predict the answer. If you were in a dream, and you knew you were dreaming…would you wake up? Or stay asleep? Think about it now. Cause once you wake up – for our people – you cannot go back to sleep! And I'd be lying to you if I said there weren't times in the beginning when I wish I could.

So, if you're still interested, pull up a seat, pour a glass or light one. 'Cause you about to find out what's up. What's REALLY up.

SLEEP

CHAPTER 1

I was born in Philly in the mid-1980s. My mother and father were neighbors but never married. My mother then met my brother's father, whom she married, and he was born in 1989. They would end up getting divorced (he had another woman), and my mother moved us to Raleigh, North Carolina in 1990. A few years later, after we moved to Durham, she went back to college and met a firefighter who would become our stepfather. **A good man. A true leader of the band embodied in the Dan Fogelberg song of the same name.** He had two children – a daughter the same age as me and a son four years older but they stayed with their mother. After she graduated, we moved to Charlotte, North Carolina for a job she accepted. My teenage years were tumultuous. Around age 15 I was sent to Raleigh to live with my grandparents and cousin who was two years older than me. I had more freedom with my grandparents, so when I was told the family was moving 20 minutes away to Wake Forest, I protested to no avail.

By the time I graduated high school in 2003, I

had gone to four elementary schools, two middle schools, and three high schools. I wasn't a straight A student. Shit, I barely made it out of high school. The first report card I brought home in the third grade was either a C or D. So, my mom knew what kind of child I would be and considered it a miracle I even graduated high school. I would later come to realize that the schools weren't teaching anything I was really interested in as far as the core classes were concerned. I did go to college briefly after high school, but once I got my license, I stopped going. It was the first time I felt I had real freedom, so, of course, I went off the deep end like most children who felt they had to sneak around their parents as a teen. I wasn't running with gangs or carrying a gun or anything like that. I was just a knucklehead. In and out of jail over dumb shit. I'm probably one of the few individuals who's been to jail twice in one day. Even the guard looked perplexed until I said "Yeah! It's me!" All over failure to appear in courts. Yeah, I was that dude.

My 20s weren't too much better. I played saxophone in grade school then picked up the acoustic guitar followed by the bass, joining a few "projects," which is a fancy way of saying I was in a band. I played shows in and around Raleigh for a few years, living the "rock star" life fueled by delusions of grandeur. I was never a solo act. I always felt I had to be part of a group to "make it." My white bandmates did not share this sentiment. They wanted me to play but didn't care for my input on writing and arranging. So, I was essentially – as Malcolm X would put it – the mascot. After I was done with music around 27 or 28, I had to look where I was. All my white friends went off and, with what seemed like ease, did other things.

I was lost for a while. My stepbrother was killed when I was 19 and I never got a chance to really know him. Now that I was older, I wished he was still around to give me some type of direction. Even though I was the eldest brother now, I needed him. I contemplated suicide, but luckily a good friend was able to help me. Shortly after that, I decided to start therapy.

I worked in the food service industry as a cook for some time. After realizing how incompetent some of my superiors were, I said to myself, "If I work for this guy, and he's an idiot, what does that say about me?" So, I got a management job. I had to wear a tie, white button-down shirt, and occasionally work a drive thru. The pay was decent, but the hours and demands were less than appealing. One day I was standing on the line (kitchen term for the area where food is made), and I looked it up and down, then out of the windows on that bright day in early December, and thought "This can't be the end of the line for me." I was bored and had grown tired of the rudimentary hustle and people of the South. I needed more. More fun. More action. More experiences.

California wasn't my first choice. At first, I wanted to leave the country. I applied to some cruise liner jobs and looked up small international off the grid communities mostly in Africa. I saw a few I liked, but I didn't have an updated passport, and I didn't want to wait 3-4 months. I had to leave sooner than that. A friend of mine had moved to the Bay Area about a year and a half prior and given me an open invitation telling me whenever I decided to come out that way, he would give me a place to stay while I got on my feet.

The days leading up to the journey were a blur. I listened to a lot of California and travel themed music. One of my favorites was "Now & Forever" on

Drake's monster album, *If You're Reading This It's Too Late.*

I wanted to do the right thing, so I put in my two weeks' notice. In the days leading up to my departure I received a pecan pie from the company and a $50 gift card only usable at the company in the mail. Now, I was a salary manager. I worked 12-hour days, 5 days a week. So, the gifts I got seemed a little lax for someone in my position. I mean, the store profits were up 6% and all I got was a crusty pecan pie and gift card. Something didn't seem right. I talked with the other managers and learned that along with the pie and gift card, they each received $300. I knew the company saw us all as expendable, and the turnover rate for the job was high. I asked the general manager about it and was told that since I was leaving, I was ineligible for the cash. So, I quit.

On New Year's Day, my mother had brunch, which was starting to become a tradition. There were a lot of people who came to wish me well. Toward the end I started to feel ill. Pneumonia set my trip back two weeks. I spent a lot of time in bed watching "Forensic Files" with my dog, a maltipoo named Murphy. It's a funny story how I got Murphy. My mom got a dog around the time I moved out when I was 21. She flew to Albuquerque, New Mexico to get him. Taking care of a puppy ain't easy, so I offered to take him for a while and told her to call when she wanted him back. She did call -- six months later. By that time, he was my dog. I had Murphy for coming up on 10 years and one of the reasons I stayed in North Carolina was because I didn't want to be away and have something happen to him. But I had to realize that I couldn't stay and wait for my dog to die.

When I got better, my mother, brother, and I went to dinner. I think she was the most excited to see me leave. She always stood by me and felt that a new environment would be good for me. She asked questions about what stops I would make and if I was excited. I told her I would first stop by grandma's and talk to her. My grandmother had been all over the world with my grandfather before his death in 2006. She had a Singapore Sling in every country she visited, the best in Spain. I then told my mom that if my cousin was there, we'd handle some unfinished business.

It was nice catching up with my grandmother.

In the middle of our discussion, the door to the back room opened, and my cousin stepped out.

Me and this nigga never got along. Since childhood, he took every opportunity to take advantage of me. Our last interaction was the catalyst. He stood in my face and called me a coward, a loser, and any other derogatory name he could spew to belittle me as a man. Well, I took that shit to the gym and was ready to come back like Clark Kent in Superman 2. When he returned from the bathroom, I went to his door and pushed it open.

"Dog! Ain't you gonna knock first?"

"Nope. We got unfinished business. Meet me out back!"

I went to the back yard and amped myself up. He was talking all that shit. Now, he was about to find out what's up! I was dead set on kicking his ass. When he didn't show up after a few minutes, I went back inside to find him. I knew he had just woke up, but I didn't give a shit. When it looked like he wouldn't bite, I started smack-talking him and calling him names. By this time, he was ready to leave and walked out the front door but quickly returned, and he was mad. We continued to yell with my grandmother in the middle trying to deescalate the situation. I followed him outside continuing to taunt him. My grandmother was trying to calm me down, but I was on a mission. This was my last task before leaving. The part of the movie where Clark goes back to the truck stop to even the score with the bully trucker who beat him up when he didn't have his superpowers. He was backing the van out of the driveway when I ran over and punched him through the open window. He stopped the van and got out talking to my grandmother explaining that I was the aggressor, which was true. And, since this wasn't a clean fight, as he stood there trying to explain, I punched him in the face.

Let me tell you something about my cousin, Tobias. He's the oldest grandchild. He ran with gangs, carried a gun in his younger days and even did some prison time. He's the smallest and hardest of the grandchildren. But it was on! I was ready to go! Payback time, muthafucka!

It didn't turn out triumphant like "Superman 2." Tobias grew up fighting and had fast hands. Jail, prison, school, job corp, the streets of west Philly and south Raleigh. I had been in some fights growing up, but it was normal kid stuff, a couple times in school and the occasional neighborhood scrap. I did have some Krav Maga training, but that was a couple years ago, and I was way out of practice. I knew there was a slim chance I'd win, but he got the message loud and clear: "I'm no longer afraid of you." I still remember him yelling "That's why you're going to California, 'cause you're a pussy!" as he drove away.

I went back into the house and looked in the mirror when I got in the bathroom. The scratches on my face were minimal and the blood on my jeans didn't come from me. My grandmother was upset and out of breath from striking us with her cane as we fought. "You don't come over here looking for a fight!" She was a witness to some of my cousins bullying and knew there was always tension between us. Then, she handed me the phone.

"You feel better?" As if he knew what was going on, my uncle James called in the middle of our scuffle.

"Yes," I replied.

It didn't take long for the word to get out in

the family about what happened. My mother called first. "Did you go over to your grandmother's house and start a fight with your cousin?"

"Yes, I told you I would."

"I didn't think you were serious! You can't get back at people that way."

"Why not?" I never understood how people could push you around, take advantage of you and expect you to take it. I know for a fact that if people could go back and get even with the people who tormented them when they were defenseless, they would. Plus, I had tried to reason with him multiple times in the past, so I spoke to him in the only language he understood. Violence.

CHAPTER 2

I ain't gonna lie - it felt good as hell to get up outta North Carolina. I had grown to hate it. There was nothing new in it for me anymore. I had done almost everything and knew almost everybody. And, if I'm being honest, I knew I would be miserable if I stayed. I mapped out my route, contacted who I needed for sleeping arrangements and left a trail of smoke.

It's an indescribable feeling to be out on the open road. The sense of restlessness and unknown exploits. Now that I look back, I don't know why I was afraid to leave.

I had a great time. Met new family and reconnected with distant ones; visited old friends; saw the Houston skyline; went to Venice Beach and the Hollywood walk of fame; gambling in Reno; museums in Memphis; Beale Street; Broadway in Nashville; the aquarium in Chattanooga; and gorgeous desert sunsets. America is a beautiful country.

CHAPTER 3

I still remember the first time I drove into the Bay. The City on one side, lit up across the bridge. Oakland on the other behind tank cars and the BART (Bay Area Rapid Transit). I felt like a country mouse.

An aunt on my Father's side had moved to the Bay Area over 20 years ago. She had a small two bedroom in Emeryville and said I could stay with her for a couple of months until I got on my feet.

I arrived the same year as the Super Bowl between the Panthers and the Colts. The game was in Santa Rosa, but Super Bowl City was in San Francisco and me, my cousin Brittany, and her boyfriend went. It may sound odd but one of my favorite things to do was to ride the train. To me, riding the train was the embodiment of living the city life. When we got up to street level, I asked her when we should smoke and she said, "We'll step off to the side before we go in." Now, I knew it was different out here but when she said "step off to the side," I didn't know that meant the sidewalk. The fact that we could stand in public and smoke weed was baffling to me. I was slightly uncomfortable until I looked around and saw that we weren't the only ones. It was relieving to live in place where the police have better things to do than jam someone up over a victimless crime.

It didn't take long to find work. The restaurant was at the corner of Harrison and 2nd Street in the Financial District. I was interviewed by the Sous chef, a Filipino guy from Texas named Jackie. During the interview he offered me $15 an hour. I asked him if my previous management experience counted for anything, but he just stared at me and repeated the offer.

I can tell ya that ya boy was making a little noise when he showed up. Being fit in the food service industry has its advantages. I did want to get with the "in" crowd but knew not to be too eager, so I focused on doing a good job.

Shortly after I started work, I fell ill. I'm guessing it was my body adjusting to the West Coast germs. The timing couldn't have been worse. My aunt got a letter from her landlord wanting to up her rent $700 because I was staying there. Now that I look back, I could tell he ain't like me. I didn't even do anything.

I was just there, making him uncomfortable being all Black and stuff. We both knew it was bullshit. She talked about fighting it but in the end, she didn't want any problems and I had to move from a bedroom to a couch. My cousin and her boyfriend (Melli P) lived on the second floor of a building owned by Melli's eldest brother. From what Brittany told me, this nigga, Van, was a cold gangster.

I had only been on the job for a couple weeks when I started to see the many problems plaguing the restaurant. The chef, Mitchell, had already checked out mentally, so Jackie had to do everything by himself. Along with the roach nest that was coming out of the salad station and no reliable night crew, he had to deal with the biased front-of-house managers and work the line, which is something a chef normally doesn't do.

There were two other guys who started when I did. One was a Latino guy named Carlos. I got along with Carlos. He was a good worker, and he cared about the job. We ended up hanging out a few times after work. I was excited to have a Latino friend. I worked with Latinos back home but never kicked it outside of work. Carlos came to San Francisco from Mexico as a kid. He did a little time in prison, but I can't recall what for. He told me a little about the city and how you ain't from the Bay if you don't love Mac Dre. He lived in the Candlestick. His place was small. The layout was practically a hallway with a bedroom at the end. It was still under his grandmother's name, so it was rent controlled. When his landlord found out she wasn't living there they wanted to double the rent on them. So, he was in a tight spot. Literally and figuratively.

It was March, but the restaurant was having a Christmas bowling party, and I knew this was a chance to get in with the waitresses.

What can I say about the Paragon crew? I met some cool people. Sprints – she was in college studying fashion. Jenny – who was super model gorgeous. Deon. Hmm, Deon. She was an interesting one, her swagger was reminiscent of Sharon Stone in *The Quick and The Dead*. Kerry - I liked her. She had a beautiful chestnut complexion. To be honest – I don't remember her nationality, but I remember that frame. Brittany – an Asian girl I shared a locker with. Mattie - she had an aggressiveness about her. This dude Daniel, who was alright. And Stephanie. Now, this was my first interaction with a white Latino. And when I say "white" I'm talking blonde hair, blue eyes white. She was full Mexican.

Something people would do is bring a change of clothes for the bar/club scene after work. The locker area at work was co-ed and some of the women would damn near change full outfits, but I kept my eyes focused on my task. If it got around that I was a creep who stared at the girls changing, it would be over for ya boy.

As I was getting in the scene with the waitresses, the restaurant was chugging along. Mitchell was gone and Jackie was taking command of the kitchen. The first thing he needed was a sous chef. Although I had never been to culinary school, I did know how to organize and cook well. When I said something to him about it, he told me that he had a friend from another job who he wanted to take the position. I couldn't be mad at him. When I was in management, I tried to look out for my friends, too.

His friend, Stanley, did not have the appearance of a professional. He was a tall, white guy with a scraggly beard and slovenly look who referred to himself as "Yeti." A goofball from Idaho. The first time he came back into the kitchen offering help he was obviously drunk. In fact, he sat at the bar in the restaurant and drank in front of everyone before coming into the kitchen. No one liked him. Of course, he was terrible at his job and only made things harder for Jackie. I could see the stress wearing on Jackie, so I told him, "You know I have management experience. I can see that you're drowning in paperwork all the time. So why don't you make me your sous chef? I can handle all the paperwork that way you can focus full time on the kitchen."

But he didn't go for it. He and Stanley came up to me a few days later and talked about training me in the back of the kitchen. "We know you're tired of working the line," Stanley said. "The line sucks." The plan was to get dependable people on the line to replace me, but it wasn't that easy. A lot of people Jackie interviewed and hired were undependable. Carlos was solid and there was a recent hire, a brother, I forgot his name. They came to work every night with good attitudes and were dependable. More important than that, we worked well together.

I came into work on a Monday and Jackie said that they both did a no call no show, which was odd because we just had drinks after work on Friday. Carlos hit up his plug for me and we were going to hit up a bar, but I had made plans to hang out with Deon. I had already stood her up once before and didn't want to do it again. So, as I walked off down the street to meet her, I glanced back at them not knowing that was going be the last time I saw them. When I asked Jackie if he knew anything he shook his head. Then he told me that Carlos had borrowed $400 to help with his apartment situation. Jackie knew he wasn't going to see that money again, so he was hella mad. I never saw Carlos again.

I had gotten in with the waitresses pretty good by now. They were all nice to me and occasionally we would get drinks after work. I was taking pictures with them, looking like the man on social media, but I wasn't sleeping with any of them. If I had played my cards right, I could've gotten with Kerry, but I decided to fumble the ball with Deon and get played by Mattie.

I was green, and Mattie used it to her advantage. I can't blame her; I went along with a lot of things that I felt I shouldn't have, trying to be considerate of her emotions. Being the good guy and doing the "right thing." Now that I look back, the signs were all there. I was unknowledgeable at the time and assumed that everyone grew up with the same morals I did. The truth is if you don't establish healthy boundaries, people will take advantage of you. And it might cost you more than you anticipated.

I came into work one night and there were a bunch of new people training, but once I took a closer look I realized most of them were drug addicts and not functional drug addicts. These were the "drugs have ruined my life" drug addicts. I was working with one guy who worked for two or three hours before saying that he wasn't feeling well and left with a burger as payment. Jackie kept telling me about his problems, so now that Stanley was out of the picture, I proposed to him to be his sous chef. Instead, he hired this guy named Nick. I didn't like him; no one did. He was a 5' 6" bald, white guy, and when he spoke, it was a slightly above a whisper. Sneaky shit. I took it personally. I can understand hiring your friend, but this was him clearly saying, "Not you."

We were able to get a couple solid hires eventually. There was Adrian. He was a tall, older, dark skin guy with a bald head probably in his 50s. I asked him if he was in the military, but he smiled and said, "No, I should've gone, though." There was also a guy named Colton. He was a tall, skinny, 27-year-old white dude (last name Lopez) with glasses and slightly crooked teeth. He had just finished culinary school on Treasure Island through a free program where he was also living. We got along well, but I soon found out that the main reason why they liked me was because I was "in" with the waitresses. Adrian once came up to me and said, "Hey man, one thing I notice about you is that you're real smooth. Like all the waitresses talk to you and you know how to talk to them. You know, just like a smooth cat!" That was the first time anyone had ever called me smooth, and I saw it kind of like a player upgrade. I would hear some of the things he and Colton would say to the waitresses, and it was comical. I got valuable advice from a woman years ago. She was very attractive and said how she hated that every guy she met would hit on her. It would be the ones who didn't hit on her that she would be more inclined to hang out with again.

Melli P was working in the warehouse/industrial kitchen of a catering company and told me that he could set me up with an interview. How it works is they send you an email asking if you can work a certain date. If you say "yes," they will send you the information about where and when to meet. My first event was at Stanford University, but the meeting spot was at the industrial kitchen. That's when I met Jeni for the first time.

Jeni was Black and Puerto Rican. She was about 5'5", maybe 125 pounds, and she was Black girl magic. I was smitten. The way her lips curved at the end of the corners of her mouth when she smiled, the way her slightly large nose sat on her face, her dark brown eyes and hair made her look like a sunflower.

One thing I enjoyed about catering was working outdoors and the constant change of scenery. They took all the equipment to the site. Tables, chairs, linens, ovens, and all. Set everything up, prepped it, cooked it, served it, then packed up and went home.

My second catering shift was at The Gallery. I met some memorable people. Bobbi was about 5' 7", mid 40s with three children. When we met, I thought she was around my age. A true testament of Black does not crack. There was also Michael Thomas. Michael was a few years older than me. A tall, dark-skinned fellow and a little odd. After the shift, Bobbi gave some of us a ride over the Bay Bridge to the West Oakland Bart Station. On the way, I explained the issue I was having with pay scale. I told her my experience and what I was being paid at the restaurant. She told me what's up and it all made sense. That's why they kept giving me raises when I asked because they didn't want to lose me. After talking to Bobbi and getting a taste of catering, I decided I was done with the restaurant. Jackie called to talk after I quit, but it was beyond that. All he had to do was pay me what I was worth from the beginning and be a straight shooter. I was there for two months.

Melli P mentioned a two-bedroom, one bathroom apartment for rent in one of the buildings his eldest brother owned. He showed me some pictures and said I'd need a roommate with the rent being $2,000/month. Not too long after, Colton called and said he was looking for a roommate.

Van was a big guy. Tall and stocky. When I talked to this man, he told me he had to start over eight times. Eight times! I was out here starting over for my third time thinking that was a lot. When he told me he had to start over eight times, it made me look at things a little differently. It made my three look insignificant. The apartment was at San Pablo and Filbert Street in west Oakland heading toward downtown. It was the hood. Drug dealers. Prostitutes. Drug addicts. I told Colton about it, but he told me his only other option was homelessness and offered to cover my portion of the security deposit. I knew it was more than I could handle, but I did it anyway.

CHAPTER 4

Melli's brother told me I was getting a deal with the price and the location, but I didn't know what the hell he was talking about. Stepping over someone shooting heroine in the doorway of the building did not seem like a deal to me. The apartment was renovated, but the repairs weren't completed. I would later find out that the building was rent-controlled and the reason we had to pay so much was because he was trying to get the old tenants out. We were the first new tenants, which is why he charged so much. The setting of the place reminded me of a tragic tale. Meth addict neighbors with a pack of dogs. The old woman who sat out front of the building and drank. The single mother who argued with her children every morning.

Colton was still at the restaurant and would tell me about Jackie having trouble keeping staff. Colton asked him about why he didn't make me his sous chef and Jackie said, "Gary doesn't even know how to make soup!"

I got some very bad advice in my teens from a guy who used to work for my father. He told me that anytime your boss asks you if you know how to do something, say "no" because if you say "yes" they'll make you do it but won't pay you extra, so I got in the habit of saying "no" to things that I'd done multiple times. He probably wasn't the best person to get life advice from.

Colton was raised by his grandmother in the northwest. She had passed away a few years earlier. He didn't have a relationship with his parents or any close relatives. He was truly out here alone. He would tell me about his interactions with the waitresses at work and ask my advice on how to talk to them.

Catering was fun. I did events in Napa Valley, San Jose, and all over the Bay. Houses, hangers, concerts, coliseums, museums, and estates. I was working one event, and we had to set up in the garage. There were bicycles hanging on the wall and just for fun I looked one up. It was $6,000. There were some events that I had to sign a non-disclosure agreement for. Ya know, in case you see a celebrity. I saw a couple but the most memorable was Chris Tucker. There were certain events that exposed me to the small pockets of wealth in East Bay. I had an event in Oakland. It was so close that I was able to walk from home. It was Pixar Studios.

I would occasionally see Jeni at events and whenever I saw a guy talking to her, I would ask her afterwards, in a friendly way, what they said. "It's always the same thing." She said casually. Then in a lower, mocking tone, "'Yo, ma! What's up! What's good!" That's when I found out women do not wanna hear that shit. I knew Jeni was highly sought after. I knew it was a long shot, but I had to try. I told her I thought we'd be good together. She was single. I was single. We both vibed well and had a history of "tokenism." I figured it was an obvious choice for both of us, but all she did was smile and nod her head or come up with some lame excuse.

Like most people, I had an online dating profile. I tried to make the quote clever because there are a multitude of options for women. I knew when dating, you had to be memorable. Something that made you stand out. Colton got discouraged after being played a couple of times, but I had to reassure him that that's how the game goes. One day I showed him my profile showing him that out of 33 women I messaged, only two chatted. One of those two women would end up being the mother of my child.

Let me start off by saying I had trepidations from the start. We met in Hayward and she walked in wearing red high heels and a black dress. She was pale and her hair was thinning. When she walked by me, my first instinct was to get up and walk out the door. But when we made eye contact, I had to stay. The place we met at was crowded for the Warriors game so, we went to a sushi place nearby. As we spoke, I learned a great deal about her. She had recently gone through a body transformation. She seemed very down to earth. After dinner, she invited me over to smoke. When I first walked in, the energy felt dark. The place was dim. Nothing in its place and dust caked on top of it. I thought to myself, "How can someone live here?" She told me her back story. It was filled with lots of trials that she was able to overcome. She got her associate's degree and backpacked through Europe. A native of the Bay Area from Modesto and no stranger to discomfort.

We were seeing each other for a week when I had a job in the city. I was standing in front of the bank with the rest of the staff preparing to unload the truck when Jeni walked up. Her hair was in an afro with a yellow flower tucked behind her right ear. During the shift I noticed she was hanging around me more than usual. I considered us friends, so I didn't read into it. But when she started touching me more – I read the signals. After work we went off and smoked. I casually asked what she was doing after and without hesitation she said, "Going with you."

We spent the whole week together.

When Jeni left, the girl from Hayward came over. When I woke up the next morning she was gone. I called and she was upset. After I tried to plead ignorance, she told me she found a ring on the floor in my room. I could've said it was my cousin's. I could've come up with any excuse, but I came clean. I told her how strongly I felt about Jeni. I remember saying, "She is me." My intention wasn't to hurt her, it was just bad timing. Ghosting her for a week didn't help.

With Jeni, it was nice to be with someone who grew up heavily into White culture like I did. She worked at a few venues in the city and Oakland and told me of some bizarre celebrity encounters. Like how

Dave Chappelle must see you open his beer before you serve it to him. We were constantly getting compliments as a couple, and I did feel more secure with her. I can honestly say I felt like I was living in an Anita Baker song. There was one instance we went to a club in downtown Oakland with a group of her close friends. It was there, while we were on the dance floor, holding each other tight when I looked up and saw a few other couples looking at us in envy. That was also when her and a close friend starting using sign language in the loud, packed venue. It blew me away. I felt like I was always learning something new with Jeni. She was an avid reader and influenced me to get a book on sign language. One day we were at my apartment and she said something about going down to the courthouse to see her mother get married. I jokingly said, "Maybe we should get married." She was quiet for a moment and stared at me before saying:

"If we get married, it's going to be for life."

"What if I wanted a divorce?" I responded with laughter. "You know, people change. We might want different things in the future."

"Nope. That's it. There is no divorce."

I quickly reconsidered the comedy aspect of my comment. Although our paths seemed to align perfectly at this moment, I knew it was too soon to make a brash decision.

Hooking up with Jeni gave me another player upgrade because a lot of guys at work tried to get with her. One night we got a ride over the bridge with some people. When one of the guys realized she was going with me, he had this look on his face. I recognized the look because I've had that same look when some other smooth muthafucka stole the girl that I was trying to get with. Now, I was that smooth muthafucka. I later asked her what made her decide to finally get with me. Her response? She was sitting around one day and thought about me. That's when I realized that's how girls shoot their shot.

As much as we got along and as head over heels in love as I was, there were a few things about Jeni's thinking that were perplexing. She had two very close friends – one Latino, the other White – and she wanted them to be my close friends, also. As honored as I was that she would bring me into her inner circle, I told her those were her friends, and just like I had a safe space to talk with my friends, she needed a safe space to talk with hers. She also let them use the word "nigga," which didn't sit right with me. When I asked her about it, she was defensive.

That was a culture shock. Non-Black people saying "nigga." I recall one brother from Texas saying, "I used to get offended, but that shit is a verb out here." Since I worked with a myriad of other races at work, I asked some of them about it and they confirmed saying, "Everybody says it out here." I had to tell them that I was from the South, and we do not play that shit. The fact that Jeni and I had to have a conversation about non-Blacks saying "nigga" was beyond irritating. I never had to explain this type of thing to anyone I dated, and I certainly didn't think I would be having this conversation with a Black girl.

Since summer was the slow season for catering, Jeni and I were feeling a financial squeeze. Luckily, she was able to get another job and return to one of her old jobs. I started looking at other things, too, which is how I came to apply for a job at a Burmese restaurant. I figured it was a long shot, but I applied and got called in for an interview. I went in and was offered a manager position in their industrial kitchen. They offered $16.50, which I felt was low, but took it anyway because I needed the job.

Things weren't looking too good for Jeni and me at this point. Jeni was on what I like to call nutty shit. What is nutty shit? It can be a few things (e.g., combativeness, ungratefulness, irrationality, being inconsiderate). We were talking once and I told her how all the Black women I dated in the past were on said nutty shit. I let her borrow my car for job interviews, did her laundry when she left it at my place, helped her with chores around her place, and she had the nerve to tell me that if I didn't like something, I could go fuck myself. She broke my heart, and I wept. It always hurt more when I broke up with Black women.

It was then that I made an unknowingly life-altering decision. I remember telling myself that I shouldn't do it. That I would regret it. The girl from Hayward came right over.

CHAPTER 5

My mother was my first visitor. She was staying with a family friend and I took them to my apartment in Oakland. Neither were fond of the neighborhood. They were slightly relieved when we got inside. The only real furniture we had was a couch that my cousin had given us and a small television on a rinky dink stand. When Neil saw we didn't have a dining table, he offered to buy one for us.

My mom was in an aerobics troupe in the early 90s. They would perform routines at malls and festivals. The leader of the dance troupe was a guy named Augustus Allen. I never understood how good of a dancer he was until I got older. Augustus was phenomenal. He danced for Patti LaBelle at the 1995 Super Bowl. I remember him being in the hospital, but I was only told that he was sick. And I remember him staying with the family for a while, but I was too young to connect the dots. Augustus passed away in Fort Lauderdale, Florida in 1997 of AIDS. His memorial was on a beach, and I vividly remember Neil walking into the ocean to release his ashes crying and hugging a close friend as he said goodbye to his lover.

Neil lived on the other side of the bridge, and as we made our way into the city to Union Square, she quickly saw the fine line between the haves and have-nots. She commented how she never knew how bad San Francisco's homeless problem was. We were at a cookout with some of Neil's friends in some prominent neighborhood outside the city when I heard the term "East Bay bottom feeders." Neil was always talking about his work and how much money he made. He teared up saying he would help me if I needed anything. He didn't like the neighborhood and said a room was waiting for me once his new house was built. I was moved by the gesture. It seemed genuine, but I declined. Despite my financial woes, I liked living on "this side of the bridge" and making my own rules. "Well, the offer is still out there if you need it. Hey! Cool shoes!" I looked over and he was pointing at my clogs.

When it to comes to possessions, sentimental things have the highest value to me. I was given a pair of kitchen clogs for men years ago by my mother. They were unique, and it was more than uncomfortable breaking them in. Neil kept going on and on about how much he liked them. I was hesitant, but since he was such a good friend of the family who I'd known since childhood, I reluctantly gifted them to him.

"What happened to that pretty girl in the picture?" my mom asked. I was so infatuated with Jeni that I jokingly sent a photo of us to the family chat saying we eloped. I told her some of what happened and how I picked her over the girl from Hayward because she was Black. I felt stupid about my decision and came to find out that there were more layers to the girl from Hayward than I expected.

I always wanted to ride a bicycle in a big city. Cutting traffic while navigating the busy sidewalks and streets. Syncing the music in my headphones with the rhythm of the city. I had started riding to the 19th street BART after buying a bicycle from what I realize now was a drug addict. He sold it to me saying "I'm an honest guy. I like to do coke and get naked."

Starting the job at the commercial kitchen was exciting. I oversaw five employees, four Latinos and a Burmese woman. On top of running the commercial kitchen, I would oversee the delivery of the product to grocers in the San Francisco and Bay Area. The orders were small, but there were multiple locations, which was time-consuming.

I was leaving work when I got a call from one of my catering jobs. The police contacted them saying that someone broke into my car. They went through my shit. Even stole my radio. I knew it was Melli's brother. He paid a crackhead to break into my car because I was behind on rent. I'm guessing the only reason I didn't get the same treatment as the neighbors (an ass kicking) was because his brother was dating my cousin. I told him about the new job and that I would pay him back, but he was tired of waiting. He wanted his money, and he decided to send a message.

The commercial kitchen was shared with a catering company owned by a Turkish woman. She was, quite frankly, a bitch. Snappy and unnecessarily aggressive. When I was introduced as the manager, she eased up, but I could tell she didn't like me. Now, I understand cultural differences. What may seem aggressive to me as an American might be the norm in other places. But, after talking to one of her employees, it was easy to conclude that she was racist. It got so bad that I had to write a statement for the company records. I saw a glimpse of how powerful the written word is during that period. Instead of telling the story over and over again, I let a coworker read the statement and her reaction was unforgettable.

I told the girl from Hayward my predicament. She said there were open rooms available at her place and although it was further away, the room would only be $500 a month. I told Colton but he didn't go for it. He didn't own a car, and Hayward was too far away for him. I told him that I never trusted Van. We were paying $2,000 a month to step over heroin addicts, then came to find out the neighbors were paying less than $1,000. I left mid-September, but still covered the full month's rent.

I don't know what I was thinking. Maybe I wasn't thinking. Maybe, my thirst for the unknown and unexplored clouded my better judgement. I didn't like the aura of the house, and I didn't see myself with her for a long time. It was supposed to be temporary until I found something else.

Now that I was staying in Hayward, I had to get up earlier for work. I would get up around 4 a.m., ride my bike three miles to BART, get off at Embarcadero, then ride another four miles to work. Looking back, it was a lot, but I was riding a bike because I wanted to, not because I had to.

When I got my paycheck, I was able to square up with Van. I gave him a hard time. Ever since we moved in, he kept saying that he was getting rid of the neighbors, but it never happened. We were also the only building on the block without a gated fence, which left us vulnerable to intrusion. I threatened not to pay but did. I remember looking at the receipt after I paid him. I was going to throw it away, but something told me to keep it. I got a call from Colton a while later saying that the roof caved in. Melli's brother didn't hire licensed contractors. He also said I never paid him.

CHAPTER 6

We were constantly on the move. Willow Grove. Fisherman's Wharf. Sausalito. Academy of Sciences. Monterey Bay. Endless adventures in and out of the city. One of the things I loved about the Bay was the parks and trails. So many you could visit a new one every week. She also spoke of interest in the underground sex scene, which was something I was interested in, too.

I knew getting into the swinger scene would be easier with a partner, but it still had its obstacles. A lot of people showed interest, but when it came down to chat or plan, there was nothing. We came up with some aliases as people do in the "lifestyle." I, Travis Legend, and she, Lexi Sweet. After multiple tries, we talked to a couple who told us about a swinger club in Oakland.

I passed by this place all the time on my way to work and had no idea it was there. We got on the guest list with the only stipulation being that we had to help clean up afterwards. Walking up, there was no one on the street except for someone standing outside the door. Inside, scantily clad people moved about multiple decorative couches and chairs. As you walk in, to the right is the bar area. Around the corner is a door that takes you outside and up a staircase to another building. One side was a large, wide-open area with cushions, beds, and benches. The other side was a BDSM dungeon. When you walk in and go to the left, there's a huge dance floor with a disco ball hanging from half of the ceiling glass. After you pass the dance floor, you go outside to a patio area. On the other side of the patio, there was a two-room building. When we walked in, our eyes were met with a mass of writhing bodies. We didn't participate that night. It was a lot to take in. The cleanup wasn't as bad as you would think. The participants were surprisingly clean.

Lexi told me stories of her tumultuous upbringing, but I would soon get a front row seat. She got a call one day about her stepbrother who was stationed in Georgia. He was in trouble for having child pornography on his computer. He claimed it was a friend of his that he didn't want to give up. I knew it was bullshit. No one takes a charge that severe for someone else. Her testimony as a character witness got him reduced time. The stepsister was a 24-year-old brat. No consideration for anyone else and got defensive any time she was held accountable. The stepfather was the worst. He'd split his time between Hayward and Weed, where the family ranch was. I'm not religious. I believe the devil is an aura. When she and I had dinner with her step grandfather and her stepfather, I knew I was sitting at the table with the devil. His disheveled look, paired with his comments about Chinese people and the way he drizzled honey on his fried chicken was enough to make me wretch. The step grandfather, Wayne, was more reserved. There was one story I will never forget. Her stepbrother had gotten very sick as a child and was hospitalized. During his time in the hospital, the father constantly complained about how inconvenient it was for him. He was never the same after that. The light in him died so to speak. At the time, I pitied him. I had somewhat of an understanding of how childhood trauma has an everlasting effect on people. I just didn't comprehend how big of an impact.

I got a call at work about a former employee who wanted to come back. He was going to take over deliveries so I could focus on the kitchen. I forgot his name, but he went to Afghanistan to spend time with the parents of his arranged wife. He had never met his arranged wife and anything he wanted to say to her had to go through the parents. This had been going on for two months. Of course, I asked him about the men over there having multiple wives and he confirmed but added, "You have to treat them all the same. If you have four wives and one has a birthday, you have to get them all gifts. You can't buy something for just one wife. It must be equal. So, you have to have a lot of money." He laughed in a Middle Eastern accent.

I was interested in marijuana culture, so Lexi and I got our medical marijuana cards. We filled out a few forms then went into a back room to see the doctor who wasn't physically there. It was an iPad on a coat stand with a medical jacket on it and he wrote us a prescription through FaceTime. The process was easy. There were a few nice dispensaries, but my favorite was The Green Room because of the upstairs lounge area.

Although we found the club in Oakland, we were still doing ads. That's how we met Lola and Starr. By the time they'd come along, we'd learned people weren't serious if they didn't Facetime. They were a mixed couple (I say mixed because interracial has a negative connotation), same as us. We met at New Parrish in downtown Oakland and after getting a good vibe from each other, Starr invited us back to his place along with another mixed couple they had come with. We knew this would be a test of our relationship. We had to shed all jealousy and insecurity if we decided to step through this door. We had to understand that what we decided to participate in was not in spite. I had to acknowledge the fact that I did not own her, and I could not put limits on her since I didn't want limits on me. We had to trust that neither of us would do anything to jeopardize our health or safety. We both consciously choose to walk through that doorway and partake in victimless pleasure. When we left, the sun was coming up.

I got an email asking me to be in a fashion show. I had been in another one a couple months prior. It was a small production run by a fashion student located near Dogpatch. Lexi and I were in the dressing room when the door swung open, and Marisa (MJ) walked in.

I'd decided to take up acting classes with a major modeling company when I relocated and that's how I met Marisa. She was gorgeous, and she knew it. Dark skin, 5' 8", thin frame. She resembled Zoe Saldana. After getting to know each other, it got to be a tradition that she and I, a Filipino girl, and a Mexican girl all went to In-N-Out after class every Sunday. They were all very pretty. I felt a strong attraction to Marisa, and I'm pretty sure she felt something too. I gave her a few good tries, but she left me hanging on multiple occasions. Nutty shit. So, I kept it moving.

When she saw me with Lexi, the disapproval in her eyes was apparent. "That's your girlfriend, huh? She's a little lighter than you, isn't she?"

"I tried to talk to you, but you kept flaking on me. I went out of my way a couple of times to meet you and you never showed." I told her about my experience with Jeni and she was shocked that I did so much for her. I would later find out that she was dating an NFL player. If she had been honest with me, I would have waited.

Now, remember when I said I took the commercial kitchen manager job even though I knew the offer was low? Well, I soon found out how low. They were paying me $10 less than the average of someone in my position. Ten fucking dollars. One of my employees was making more than I was! The lawsuit against the company involving mistreatment of worker labor made complete sense now. It was a tough lesson on the importance of negotiating. When they made the offer, I didn't push back. I just accepted the scraps they threw at me. No negotiating. Why? I desperately needed the job and I didn't know my value. Of course, they used rhetoric when I confronted them. Different pay scale, blah, blah, blah. I knew what they were doing was wrong, but I didn't know enough to fight back. And they knew it, which is why they did it. They fired me the following Monday through email. I got fired on my day off, just like Craig.

I was able to go back to catering, but it was still the slow season. I busied myself by going to the gym and cleaning up the foliage and debris around the house, which was way, way overdue for maintenance. Not only did no one in the house help, they said nothing. No appreciation or recognition. I had never had inconsiderate roommates, so it was an adjustment.

Lexi's stepsister constantly had people over. Throwing parties and not cleaning up. Having people stay in the living room all weekend. She never said anything. She just did it. We had gotten two other roommates since I moved in. Young guys who were just as unkempt as her. I can only imagine the lies she told them about me, and it was soon apparent that they sided with her when it came to house issues. All I wanted was some consideration. The stepfather would come stay occasionally, and Lexi was tasked with telling him about the charges his son was facing. He cried like a baby.

A short time later, I got a call from my mother. My grandmother had booked a flight to Las Vegas without telling anyone. That would've been fine if she didn't have multiple sclerosis and occasionally used a wheelchair. Since work was slow, she asked if I could go. Las Vegas for four days? Hell yeah! Lexi came along. This wasn't my first trip with my grandmother. When I was 11, she took me and a cousin to Europe. Years later, we went to our first Comic Con together.

Gambling, casinos, nice restaurants, drinking on public streets, marijuana dispensaries, roof top pools and bright lights. On the third day, I got a call around 10 a.m. It was a paramedic telling me that my grandmother had driven down the steps at the Palazzo on her scooter. When I made it down there, she was being put into the ambulance and told me what happened. In the Palazzo, the ramps alternate from side to side with steps in-between. She had gotten a gelato and while eating, she forgot to switch sides and took her scooter down the small amount steps. I've called her "Vegas buddy" till this day. We had a great time and by the fourth day, I was ready to leave.

Although Lexi and I were having a good time, I did notice some cultural differences, but that was to be expected. One weekend she wasn't feeling well because she had a cold. I told her to rest, but she refused, saying that when you're sick it's best to keep moving so your body doesn't succumb to the illness. So, ignore it until it goes away. That made absolutely no sense to me. I was always taught that when you're ill, you stay home and rest your body. Plus, you don't want to spread your illness, right?

By now, Lexi's stepbrother had finished his time, which was suspiciously short. When I saw him there was no doubt in my mind that he was guilty. He filled in all the boxes. He was standing in the hallway in his grandmother's pajama pants, gut hanging out, glasses and military haircut that made his head look like a pencil eraser. A virgin in his mid-20s who spent most of his time in front of a computer screen. He never thanked his sister for being a character witness. Never said a word. He was an exact copy of his father.

I knew I was dancing a fine line when it came to Lexi and her family. Like I said, it was supposed to be a good time not a long time. When Lexi came to me and said she was pregnant, I still didn't grasp the severity of the situation. I was fully immersed in a fantasy world. I was actually happy when she told me.

Have you ever felt a wave of relief? That WHOOSH feeling? When the doctor told us she'd had a miscarriage it snatched me out of that fantasy world. The big, flashing exit sign that says, "Get off here, nigga, 'cause the road you're on is about to fuck you up."

CHAPTER 7

At the time, I didn't understand the unhealthy ways people cope with trauma. I naively thought it was general knowledge that when you experience something extremely traumatic, you take time to grieve, cope, and most importantly work through your trauma. If you don't, those emotions will seep out. It may take time, but they will seep. The result? Bleeding on people who didn't cut you. Unfortunately, most of the time, those people are your significant other and/or your children.

After the miscarriage, the doctor told Lexi to rest. Instead, she scheduled a photoshoot. The following day she wasn't feeling well enough for work. We went to the emergency room at St. Rose Hospital and after some bloodwork, she was released with a prescription for painkillers. A few days later, she wasn't any better, so we went to Stanford Health Care.

I didn't know it at the time, but when you have health insurance, some doctors will send you to their doctor buddies to get a cut of the insurance money. We had to go to four doctors before it was discovered that she had a blood infection. Her white blood cell count was five times higher than normal. The fourth doctor told us that if we didn't come to him when we did, she probably wouldn't have lived through the week due to organ failure.

Now, I'm not a medical professional but I do have common sense. She was fine until she returned from the photoshoot with a cut on her ankle. During our multiple hospital visits I told each doctor about it, and they all dismissed me. These "medical professionals" took all these tests and not one looked at the obvious abnormality in her blood work. And wouldn't you know, the cut was the answer all along. That goddamn cut was the start of one of the most painful growing experiences of my life. That small cut taught me about myself, Lexi, her family, the medical industry, and false modesty.

Lexi's photoshoot was at a former mineshaft and river in East Bay called the Secret Sidewalk. It's not uncommon for people to walk dogs or ride horses there. Well, someone was riding their horse on the trail and the horse defecated in the water. The high heels she wore had spikes around the heel and she cut herself as she was taking photos. Water splashed in the cut resulting in sepsis. She spent two days in the emergency room, four days in ICU, three weeks in the hospital, and two weeks in a nursing home.

Her family was of no help. They made the situation about themselves. All that mattered to them was how they perceived the situation. It was all about them and their emotions. Focusing on my actions and what I did wrong. It didn't matter that the stepsister saw Lexi painfully walking down the hallway in the house wearing a leg brace and using a cane and decided to close her bedroom door instead of asking what's wrong. It didn't matter that the stepbrother saw me walk into the house for the first time without her and didn't say anything. It didn't matter that her mother only came to hospital when I told her my parents were coming from across the country. And it didn't matter that I was the only person out of five paying rent and straightening up the house. There was zero accountability on their end. Everything was my fault. Lexi's stepfather and stepbrother tried to jump me her first night in intensive care. The stepsister called the police, and I had to leave.

I called Neil. After all, he offered to help me and seemed sincere. He never got back to me, and I had to live in a hotel for six weeks. I decided then that I would never give away something that was given to me by my mother.

It was a lot for me to take, and I broke down more than once. But I can't lay all the blame on them. They were being their true selves and at the time, and I saw the best in people. I had the chance to walk away but didn't. I didn't listen to myself. I was more concerned with Lexi. I wanted to be the "good guy" and do the noble thing.

CHAPTER 8

With the help of my parents, we were able to find a one-bedroom apartment in Union City. The experience with Lexi's family stirred my sleep but didn't fully wake me. It did make me more cognizant of how people responded to us as a mixed couple. Like the woman in the leasing office. She was cordial until she saw Lexi's drivers' license. I watched her demeanor change, and she assigned us a parking spot that was practically on the opposite side of the complex.

Lexi had a painful recovery. She needed five blood transfusions, a couple surgeries, and she had to learn to walk again. It's not easy to watch someone you care for go through what she went through. The crying, pleading, and feelings of helplessness. When it got around at work, a lot of people were shocked that I decided to stay. I couldn't see why. It was the right thing to do, wasn't it?

Her mother brought us some furniture she purchased at a yard sale, and when I finished unloading she just stood there, looking at me. I don't know if she was waiting for a "thank you" or an invitation to stay but she got neither. I was still upset about what went down. Not only was I jumped by her husband and son, but when I told her that her husband swung at me first, she didn't believe me! I was livid! I said the meanest thing I could think of: I told her that she was a terrible mother, and if I were her child, I'd kill myself. Her mouth hung open and she claimed I "attacked" her. I never told Lexi that she couldn't see her mother or have her mother over to the apartment. I just didn't want to be around when she did. The events that occurred are not something you just sweep under the rug. Until she was ready to talk about it, I wanted nothing to do with her.

I didn't understand at the time how difficult it is for people to apologize. Most people give gifts, which isn't wrong, but an apology takes humility. Acknowledging your faults and recognizing the areas where improvement is needed are important on the path to personal growth.

I was already in a lot deeper than I'd intended. I'd signed an 18-month lease so the rent would be cheaper, thinking we'd separate when the lease ended. I didn't forget how excited she was about the pregnancy. So, I had to be sure that I did not get her pregnant again.

It was exhilarating for us both to escape the sinister and gloomy aura of the house on Swift Court. Peace at home is paramount to mental health because if you can't be happy at home, where can you be happy? With her unemployment (she was unable to return to work) and my pay, we were able to make rent. Her mobility wasn't the same. I called a few lawyers about a possible medical malpractice lawsuit, and one sent paperwork. I told her to write down her experience. We went through a lot of unnecessary traumas due to the neglect of multiple doctors. She almost died and was left with permanent scarring by one of the doctors who drained fluid on her shoulder, but she never wrote it down. It could've been a nice payout, too.

We enjoyed our "shag pad" as my dad called it. We did puzzles and watched movies. Took day trips and went out for dinner. We hosted a few swinger parties. Lola and Starr were our go-to couple. Starr was very plugged into the scene, and we met new people from all walks of life. Some who knew porn stars. We also met Carol and Dennis.

Carol and Dennis were former Mormons and if I had to guess, this was a last-ditch effort to save their marriage. They were a mixed couple. She was White and he was Mexican American (one parent from Mexico and the other from New Mexico). They had grown up in Mormonism and were married young. They did everything their religion told them to. He finished school and made good money as an accountant at a law firm while she stayed at home and raised their five children. It had been like that for almost 20 years. By the time we met them, they were almost fully immersed in the lifestyle. My interaction with them taught me a lot about the importance of knowing yourself as an individual. When people get married at a young age and haven't had the chance to explore and discover who they are as an individual, it's only a matter of time before the longing to discover themselves can't be contained. They will lash out, sometimes in destructive ways, in their quest for individuality and self-discovery. Unfortunately, Dennis and Carol eventually divorced. Dennis and I hung out on occasion. I liked Dennis, as he reminded me of myself. A nice guy with good intentions, but his over enthusiasm to make new friends made him vulnerable to deception.

Like I said earlier, I wasn't fully awake, but I was paying more attention. For instance, at work, I began to see the confidence other cultures carried. The company needed drivers to shuttle the staff to some of the events and drivers got paid an extra $2 an hour. I didn't think about doing it until an event in San Jose when one of the drivers locked the keys in the van. He was a kid, maybe 19 or 20 years old. That was when I thought to myself if he can do it, (and he's an idiot) I know I can.

I did make some downright stupid decisions. Lexi had a DUI charge from 7 years ago. The rate for car insurance would be much cheaper under my name even though it was her car (the tags had expired on my car. I tried to fix it but every time I went to get it inspected, I was told I needed to drive it more to pass emissions). Instead of getting insurance like I was supposed to (because I was so confident in my driving skills), I bought another bike. I've never hit a deer, but sure enough as I was driving across the Hayward bridge after work at 4 a.m. I did, which was strange because deer aren't usually around that area. I was able to drive back to the apartment, but when I came out the next morning, the car was gone. Towed.

Lexi's step grandfather used to be in business with the guy who owned the towing company. I got there and this very large Latino woman was sitting behind the desk. She didn't look happy. When I asked her about the car and told her who I was, she didn't care. But when Lexi showed up, everything changed. I didn't like the guy. He had Klan member vibes. We went back to his office and explained what happened to see if he could help. After our conversation, it was apparent that he only wanted to help himself. He told me to get insurance and wait a few days to file the claim. His plan was for me to tell them I got into an accident in Modesto and that he towed me back (even writing a fake receipt) so he could make money off the tow. I knew it wouldn't work. Insurance claim adjusters aren't idiots, and I know I'm not the first person to try this. Lexi, the guy at the body shop, and her mother did what was necessary to alter any documents. The hardest part for me was the lying. I didn't like doing it.

Of course, it didn't work. I had never been to Modesto and the adjuster knew it because he didn't see me on any traffic cameras. Luckily, we didn't face any harsh repercussions. I remember riding my bike to the BART station for work thinking, "Good job, dummy. You went for the bike instead of insurance and now you're riding it to work because you have to." A few weeks later, they found a replacement vehicle for us. I could tell the owner of the body shop was waiting for something, but I didn't feel like I owed him anything. We came to him for help, and he looked out for his own interests.

Every so often I would hear about Lexi's family. Her stepfather was a blundering idiot. He always had some harebrained scheme that never panned out. For example, he attempted to be a beekeeper and thought it would be a good idea to have a bee sting him so he would become immune to the venom and wouldn't have to buy safety gear. The picture of him with a huge bee sting on his face was comical.

Her mother was still upset I wasn't being cordial. She would tell Lexi, "We're family, if he's going to be with you, he's going to have to accept us also." In my opinion, that's a statement made by toxic people. People who do you wrong and continue to do you wrong because you are family. As if you are designated to carry extra weight they knowingly put on you because of blood ties.

My mother gave me a book before I left. *A Choice of Weapons* by Gordon Parks. I don't recall why I put it in my backpack. The back of the bag was mesh, and anyone could see that I was carrying a book, so I guess it was kind of a social experiment. I was at a job one day and as we were all in the elevator getting ready to leave, someone asked, "What you readin' on, playa?" I had only read the back and I told him the small amount I knew. I had a lot of commute time, and I stopped listening to music while walking through the city. There was so much going on I wanted to be cognizant of my surroundings. So, I started reading.

I would find out that there were a lot of similarities between my journey and that of Gordon Parks. Similarities that would show me that the path I was on and the experiences I had were not unique. There were countless Black men, like me, who were lost and confused. One thing that stood out to me was the end: When he returned home with these new "weapons" and used them to help and educate his people.

One evening at work the subject of smoking came up. One of the older guys told me he's a former smoker. He laughed as he recalled his brother giving him a hard time on the basketball court when he would tire quickly and how a girl told him once "Ya know, you're too cool to smoke." He told me about *The Easy Way to Quit Smoking* by Allen Carr. The book was very informative. It told of how cigarette companies pay movie productions to have their products in films to attract more customers. Specifically, young, impressionable teenagers and adolescents. And how the cigarette industry spends less than 10 percent of its revenue on anti-smoking ads created by people who were never smokers.

I started following a pro-Black page on social media, which led me to my next book, *Forty Million Dollar Slaves: The Rise, Fall, and Redemption of the Black Athlete* by William C. Rhoden. I never cared too much about sports. I enjoyed playing and being a spectator, but I never had a "team." Fawning over the accomplishments of professional athletes was always foreign to me. Upon learning of Major Taylor, Tom Molineaux, Isaac Murphy, Moses Fleetwood Walker, Arthur "Rube" Foster, and Gus Greenlee, I was able clearly see the lengths "the establishment" went through to keep the major accomplishments and contributions of MY people hidden. I was taking in a lot of information that began to make me question what I had been indoctrinated to believe about my people, my culture, and my place in society.

I've known Steven since high school. He's solid. In all our years of friendship, he never mentioned my color. He's told me of the people in our so-called "friend circle" who've made racial epithets when I wasn't present, and he would correct them. When I made my first return trip home in 2017 for a family wedding I got in contact with his girlfriend (now wife), telling her that I would be coming and wanted to surprise him. When he opened the door, the look on his face was exactly what you'd expect from a great friend of over 15 years. I caught him sitting on the edge of his bed weeping as we got ready to go downtown that night. I told him to stop, or I would start crying, too. When he called to say he was coming to visit, it was just what I needed to take my mind off things. Sausalito, Jack London Square, downtown Oakland, the mission, music venues, hippie hill on 4/20, Lake Merritt. By the time he left I was exhausted, but I'd do it again.

WOKE

CHAPTER 9

Do you remember sleeping at a cousin's house as a child and playing pranks on each other? Did you have a cousin pour water on you while you were asleep? That's what waking up was like for me. I was sleeping good. Mouth open. Drooling. Snoring.

It was a trickle at first. Then the emptying of the bucket made me shoot up, gasping for air. Lost in a space of confusion and shock. I'd be lying if I said it didn't suck. It. Fucking. Sucked. I called my mom frantic, and she said, "Okay. Calm down. What you are experiencing is called 'woke'." I remember it like it was yesterday.

Whenever there is a black man without knowledge, there's always going to be a white man to take advantage of him.

-Unknown

There's a book called *The Mis-Education of the Negro* by Carter G. Woodson. My mother had a copy in the house. When I was around 10 years old, my mom briefly dated a guy who had lots of books and comic books. He told me to read *The Mis-Education of the Negro*, and I would get a prize in return (I don't remember what it was). At the time, I liked reading. Now that I look back, that book was way too advanced for a fifth grader. I was eager to start but didn't get far into it. I just didn't get it. I didn't understand the concept. I do remember one thing it said. "When you control a man's thinking you do not have to worry about his actions. You do not have to tell him to stand here or go yonder. He will find his 'proper place" and will stay in it. You do not need to send him to the back door. He will go without being told. In fact, if there is no back door, he will cut one for his special benefit." It made sense now. I had become just that.

It all made sense. Every questionable interaction, uncomfortable situation, backhanded compliment, nasty look, and sly remark. I then thought about all the "silent alarms." I remember a few quite well but it didn't paint the full picture for me. Subtle clues given by other Blacks that were often presented in the form of an insult. Back home, I was the token. That Black guy thinking he was making a difference by having a crowd consist of mostly Whites. I always knew I was Black, and I knew racism and prejudice were out there, but I assumed it was blatant. And when I did encounter it, I just accepted it and moved on. I used to believe that the negative experiences I was having with non-Blacks were isolated events. After I read *A Choice of Weapons,* I realized that this was untrue. No matter how I saw myself and how much I tried to fit in and be accepted, I was just a nigga, and I would never be fully accepted by people who weren't my people. It didn't matter how many times I saw Marilyn Manson in concert. It didn't matter that I knew the television show *Friends* almost back to front or that I liked Kiss and Lady Gaga. I mean, these people talked and drank and laughed with me. Shared the stage with me in our mutual love for music. I assumed it genuine, right? After all, racism and prejudice were fading away, right? The thoughts of the previous generations, right? WE were making progress, right? I can't judge all non-Black people because I've had a few negative interactions, right? I mean, there are marches and films and television shows about cultural unity and peace. That's progress, right?

I had myriad questions but no answers. I also had to realize the situation I had put myself in. Not only did I wake up, but the person who I was in a relationship with did not see what I saw, feel what I felt, and could not identify with me on a level that I started to yearn for. I always felt Lexi was solid but when I asked, "If you were in a dream and you knew you were dreaming, would you choose to continue dreaming? Or would you choose to wake up?" Her answer made me understand how much trouble I was in.

I became fascinated with reading. I read anything that piqued my interest. Marcus Garvey and the Pan African movement; Gary Webb and the CIA's involvement with the importation of cocaine; the military's practices during the Iraq and Afghanistan Wars; spotting deception within others through body language and behavior; the book *Pimp* by Iceberg Slim. The odd thing was, the more subjects I read about, the more pieces fell into place. One of my favorite shows was *The Shield* (a TV drama about corrupt police in Los Angeles), and when I heard it was loosely based on real events, I had to find out more. This led me to one of the most informative books I have ever read, *The Thin Blue Line* by Matthew B. Gordon. The book explains the "us vs. them" mentality of the police along with their credo, "If you watch someone long enough, they'll do something illegal." It also outlines the two types of policing. You have reactive policing, which leads to police brutality, and community policing, which leads to police corruption.

I had to dance a fine line when it came to my intake of knowledge. Because of my situation there were some rabbit holes I had to avoid, lest I discover something that would subconsciously make me resent Lexi and the white people I had come to call friends out here.

I knew to dodge El-Hajj Malik El-Shabazz. I knew to dodge Louis Farrakhan. I even knew to scroll past Khalid Abdul Muhammad. None of these guys had anything to say about mixed relationships that would ease my mind. But one Black leader I didn't see coming was The Prince of Pan-Africanism. King Kong Consciousness himself, Dr. Umar Johnson, who said, "I don't care who you name, I don't care how much work you did for Black people. Your greatest commitment to Black people is being committed to a Black woman. It is still a contradiction. No matter how much you think you did for the struggle. If you really were concerned with Black people, you would've committed yourself to a black woman. So, it doesn't matter how successful they are, it doesn't matter how great you may claim them to be. At the end of the day, you didn't think enough about your own people to marry a woman that looks like you."

I noticed a change in behavior toward me when I was seen reading a book. People, in particular Whites, seemed to be perplexed at the sight of a Black man reading. Like seeing a bear ride a unicycle. Even my coworkers would make comments when they saw me reading that would show their uncomfortableness and feelings of inferiority, mostly through laughter. Then, there was that time I was out with coworkers. About nine of us went to a bar after work. I noticed that when I spoke, they listened intently. So, I read more.

It wasn't too much later I noticed the portrayal of Black men in major movies and television shows. What I read about us, from us, and what I was shown was a complete contradiction. Rarely the hero; always dealing with some internal conflict; homosexual; dating a non-Black woman; cross dressing; the comedic relief who's never taken seriously; needing the help or advisement of some White savior; making sacrifices to aid White characters; a hoodlum; womanizer; slave. Then I noticed the White characters. Noble and honorable; wise; steadfast; always able to conquer obstacles and inner insecurities, allowing the viewer to gush as they rise to victory. But, more importantly, no matter how much harm the White character had done or how much trouble they caused, they either get away or die the hero. I concluded that this had an impact on the minds of Whites, and I watched them more intently. I began to understand how they had been trained to see the best in themselves. Seeing constant positive representation of themselves gave them a false sense of empowerment and entitlement. Crazy, right? But then I had to ask; If it's not true, then why whitewash roles? Making films about Egyptian kings, queens and gods that are portrayed by Whites but using Black actors to portray slaves. Or taking true stories and whitewashing characters or adding White fictional characters? I remember going out of my way a few times to help some White friends of mine back home and they showed no gratitude in return. But after all, I am supposed to help them. I had seen myself do it multiple times in film and television. Trained to care more about them than myself. And they let me. After a while, it got to a point where if I didn't like the representation or if there was no representation of myself, I wouldn't watch it.

Then I thought, "What if I switched it around? Instead of seeing the best in others, what if I assumed that they were mostly bad and only some good? After all, aren't those the rules they are playing by?" I mean, at first glance, to them, I was the "scary" or "ignorant Black," and I unknowingly went out of my way to let them know I was "safe." I then made a life-changing decision: I would no longer cater to the egos of those who did not look like me to ease their discomfort.

The more I read, the more I began to reflect and understand the subtle racism, passive aggressiveness, and prejudice I'd encountered in my past. In my English class my senior year of high school, we had to write a chapter of a story each week and present the finished product at the end of the year. I wrote three stories: mine and two for some friends at a price. I put effort into mine and rushed through the others. My book, which was the thickest out of every book in every class, got me a "B." The White girl for whom I wrote a rushed story full of typos, got an "A."

The teacher who brought in his black rabbit named him "B.B.," an abbreviation for black bastard. When he told me, I threw my head back and laughed.

How I was used in the local music scene for my talents but brushed off when attempting to present ideas. How I joined one group with a few older guys and when I discovered one to be a proud racist from Brooklyn, I learned the other two members knew all along but hid it from me. How someone listed my misdemeanor at 18 as a felony, which made me miss out on jobs until my mother called and told them to fix it. That could have seriously hindered my life if she hadn't stood up for me.

I also had to reflect on my dating history. I dated both Black and White women. I realized that whenever I was hurt or rejected by a Black woman, I went right back to White women. I had to ask myself why. I've had multiple encounters with rude or prejudiced White women but always said, "It's ok. They're not all like that. I'll just move on to the next." But when it came to Black women, I would lump them together and assume they were alike. I had to understand I was lying to myself. For a long time, I didn't think Black women liked me. But once I really thought about it, it just wasn't true.

I remember Black girls liking me as far back as middle school. Some whom I'm sure turned into real baddies. Whenever I dated a Black woman, it was like electricity flowing through my body. But there always seemed to be miscommunication somewhere. But maybe they had been successfully programmed to resist and dismiss me the way I had been programmed to overlook them. Now that I had begun to see the subliminal messages, I had to look at the messages Black women are given.

Only Black women are given the message that they must be strong and independent. Songs about scrubs, hittin' 'em up, men being replaceable and expected to pay their bills seem to be directed only to Black women. We're flooded with images of the brash, loud, combative, neglectful, violent, sexually objectified Black woman who declares that she sees no value in a Black man aside from his income or ability to please her sexually. Confrontational when opposite Black men but passive when opposite non-Black men and her life would be more fruitful with a white man. Maybe, just like me, they didn't know. Unaware of the Black female pioneers and their immeasurable contributions in our history: Bessie Coleman; Sarah Baartman; Ester Jones; Selma Burke; Hattie McDaniel; Rosetta Thorpe; Bessie Stringfield; Fannie Lou Hamer; Henrietta Lacks; Shirley Chisholm; Surya Bonaly; and countless others.

I then came across a video clip that made me come to another realization: Black women are the only women who have to limit themselves for the comfort of others.

"This brother here, myself, all of us were born with our hair like this and we just wear it like this. All of them because this is natural. Because the reason for it - you might say - is like a new awareness among Black people that their own natural appearances, physical appearance, is

beautiful and pleasing to them... For so many, many years we were told that only White people were beautiful - only straight hair, light eyes, light skin is beautiful. And so Black women would try everything they could, straighten their hair, lighten their skin, to look as much like White women... But this has changed because Black people are aware now...and White people are aware of it too because White people now want natural wigs. They want wigs 'like this.' Dig it? Isn't it beautiful? Alright!"

-Kathleen Cleaver

I also noticed how the Black woman is the least protected woman in society. The last to receive aid or be shown compassion. The trends they set and responsibility for innovations across various professional fields with little to no recognition. They are the only ones who've shown unwavering support for the Black man during slavery, the civil rights era, and today. I began to see Black women for what they are. Phenomenal. The ever impressive, the long contained, the always imitated but never duplicated

Black woman.

I decided that I would create my own "code" when it came it my people. I would see all Black people as a collective. I would no longer look at another Black man as a threat but as a reflection. I would no longer attack (verbally or physically) another Black person. I would no longer speak ill of my people in the presence of non-Blacks. If I overheard a coworker speaking ill of a Black coworker, I would tell them. I had been successfully trained to see a Black man and assume the worst. I finally understood that other people looked at me the same way.

AWARE

CHAPTER 10

I would soon find out that not all Black people shared the same mindset. I had a few conversations that numbed my enthusiasm about connecting with my people. While working an event in Fort Mason, I met a brother about my age who was from the South. He told me that he had become more pro-Black since moving away from home. As we spoke, I was able to tell him all the thoughts I had pent up inside. Once, when he saw my demeanor change after a non-Black coworker said "nigga," he jumped in to calm the situation.

"But how else are they going learn?" I asked him.

"Why do you care?"

"Why don't *you* care?!" I fired back as we sat in my truck in front of his apartment in Alameda. "That's exactly what they expect from Black people! They expect us not to care 'cause niggas don't give a shit about shit! All we care about is fucking bitches and getting money that we're going to spend with other cultures who don't even like us! Look around! Ain't nobody pretending to be Indian or Mexican or Arab! They are all pretending to be us! Using our words, listening to our music, dancing like us and walking like us. These are the same people who take every facet of our culture but still see YOU and ME as a couple of dumb niggers cause that's the question when talking to a non-Black: Do you see me or just a nigger? We are the scapegoats of society. The fall guy. They look down on us but take everything we have and give us nothing tangible."

"What about Black history month?"

"What about it?"

"They lookin' out, right?"

"Nigga..." I said as I laughed and rubbed my forehead. "What else happens during Black History Month?" I held up my hand to give him a visual. "You got the NBA All-Star Game. Then what? The Super Bowl. Then what? The Oscars. And after that, the Grammys. Those events overshadow the whole month. A distraction! Cause yeah, some Black guy just got killed, which could easily be me or you, but the Warriors are in the playoffs! Pay attention! Do you know who Major Taylor is?"

"No."

"Major Taylor was the first Black man (although he was 12) to win palindrome races in the early 1900s. I saw a commercial that referenced him and guess what the product was."

"What?"

"Hennessy, nigga! Here is a monumental figure in our culture that wasn't taught to you or me in school, and his image is being used to sell alcohol 'cause everyone knows niggas love Hennessy," I said mockingly.

"We're not the only ones. Other races have it hard, too."

"That's true. We are all in the same storm, but we are not in the same boat and when it's time, they will remind you of that. We are not accepted. We are tolerated."

"So, what would make you happy? What do you think needs to be done?"

"Honestly, bruh, what would make me happy is seeing us everywhere. A place where we can truly feel comfortable, like our own territory. I want to go downtown and see nothing but Black people."

There was another guy I met from the gym. I was in the locker room when he asked me about my headphones. I knew it was an attempt to create friendship, and I went along with it. I met him for coffee one afternoon in Castro Valley, and he asked how I was doing. Since he was Black too, I told him. "Wow! I did not see that coming," he said calmly with a look of shock on his face. I soon saw a pattern develop. When I saw myself in another Black man, I would try to empower him with the importance of reading, but they all smiled, nodded, and then kept their distance from me. I can imagine I sounded like a Black militant radical. I just wanted them to care. I then decided to internalize my thoughts until I met someone who was also knowledgeable.

I met Stephanie through work around that time. A Black woman about nine or ten years older than me who was a military brat from the South and an only child. She was previously married to a White man but knew Black history, which was a topic I was most interested in. We were on the same frequency. I got something while I was around her that I forgot about, the sense of being and security that come with being with a Black woman. We were getting off work one day and went into a store together. Some random White woman walked clear in front of her, cutting her off and she snapped on her. "You don't see me here? Y'all think you can get away with whatever, but you gonna learn." The woman walked away shocked. "See? I can't be going places with you. I be ready to jump on people," she said smiling. I knew exactly how she felt. I could tell she did not like the fact that I was with a White girl. I told her that I woke up while in a mixed relationship. Lexi and I were so intertwined that I couldn't just leave. She was a good woman. The only reason why I would be breaking up with her is because she's White. Would that make me racist? She, like me, was growing increasingly frustrated with constantly feeling out of place. Not too long after, she got offered a management position, but it didn't last. She told me she felt that she wasn't given all the tools to correctly do her job and felt more harshly critiqued than the other managers. We talked about it before she took the job and how there were no people of color in upper management. There were Latinos but they were very fair skinned and could pass for White.

I would find out that most Black people were uncomfortable in most spaces. When I worked events (which were majority White or non-Black) I would look for other Black people. Getting in a small huddle and saying, "I was hoping to see some of us." Or the woman at the train station who saw me reading James Baldwin and told me how angry she was that our contributions to this country were kept from us. Or when I went to a farmers' market and when an older Black gentleman made eye contact with me, he came over and smiled saying, "I'm glad to see you. I be feeling like an endangered animal sometimes when I'm out here." It was nice knowing that I wasn't alone. A feeling I had become accustomed to. I was walking to a job with a coworker one day and he asked, "Do you ever feel bad sometimes? I'll be places where I'm the only Black person, and I'll feel bad for being there."

"I used to. Now that I have more knowledge of self and know the truth, I don't feel that way anymore. This country owes us everything. People use inventions every day that were created by Black people. Everyone imitates, but we are the original. They love our culture; they just don't love us." I then stopped and looked at him. "There's a reason they don't want niggas to read."

By this time, the killings of unarmed Black men by police were all over the news. I was struggling mentally. Sometimes, it felt like my brain was splitting in two and other times it felt like I was in a virtual reality. I was still meeting Lexi's family, and although they smiled to our faces, their choice of words and body language exposed their real thoughts. They were uncomfortable looking at us, and they felt she lowered herself by being with me. I would find out that in White culture, marrying or dating someone who isn't White is considered a downgrade. I could tell Lexi was uneasy about how much I was reading, saying things like, "You should be careful. That stuff can affect your brain."

I was in Sacramento when Stephon Clark was killed. I was standing outside when I saw another brother and asked him his thoughts about what's happening. I got more than I bargained for when he opened his mouth. "You see that over there?" he asked, pointing across the street to a boarded-up store front. In the corner, in graffiti, it said "Moscow." "I saw that overseas during the war. Something's coming. All these people have the wrong idea. They're buying guns and ammunition, but they don't know how to shoot. Not in a combat zone. When it hits, people are going to be in trouble and all these Blacks in mixed relationships are gonna have to pick a side."

Although I was in the early stages of consciousness, I was yearning to have an intellectual conversation. The conversation came from someone who I didn't expect: Starr. Lexi and I went over to see him and Lola one evening when I noticed something I hadn't before. Starr was well traveled and well known in the swinger community, but his extensive book collection was what made me envy him. So much knowledge at his fingertips. Starr was from Africa and knew that Black Americans were miseducated about American and world history. I told him that America should tell "the truth" and right the wrongs that were done against us. "Like the Germans and the Holocaust. They acknowledged what they did was wrong and corrected it. America needs to do that!"

"Yeah, but only because they're White." He then told me of the genocide by the Germans against the Herero tribe of South-West Africa. "The Germans wiped out 80 percent of them. And this was before the Holocaust. You don't hear about that, do you? Or King Leopold II of Belgium who was responsible for the death of over 15 million Africans in the Congo. But they'll condemn Hitler. Ya see?" At the end of our conversation, I asked him for a good, mind-bending book. He got up, walked over to a shelf, and came back with Frantz Fanon's *The Wretched of the Earth*. "I think you'll like this one."

One evening I was having a bad day (which was common at the time) walking through the apartment complex. These two guys walking across the way were talking. As they got closer, I could make out some of the words. One kept saying he's been having a bad day and he's ready to fight. My ears perked up. I had been angry for some time and a fight was just what I wanted. "I'll fight you. I've been having a bad day too. I got some gloves. And I don't like the fact that y'all be sayin' nigga when y'all ain't niggas. So, let's go!"

"Oh! You're the one!" A couple weeks ago I had heard a neighbor stand on his balcony saying "nigger" with impunity. I never saw him because of the layout of the apartment, but I knew he wasn't Black. I spoke with another neighbor about it, and he said something to them. "You can't be getting mad. That's how people talk out here." After some back and forth, I started to feel bad. Then, something strange happened. I realized that they were scared. I was like a riled-up pit bull they were trying to calm. I spent more time talking with them and got a more in-depth look at how the people who siphon our culture think. It was only when the night guard showed up, a younger Black guy, who also said he didn't like non-Blacks using the word, did they begin to understand. That's when it hit me: all these non-Blacks saying nigga don't know any real niggas.

Despite my best efforts, Lexi got pregnant. I asked about birth control, but she had stopped taking it. As distraught as I was, I saw it was coming. She wasn't working and was home a lot by herself. By this time, I was able to understand how impactful a child's environment is when growing up. There was too much damage and no matter what I did, it would never be enough. I was unable to reason with her and certain issues never got resolved. While I was out here exploring, she was running away. She never wanted to confront a problem and saw criticism as an attack. When we first met, she talked about getting into therapy but that's all it was – talk.

I had already made up my mind that she would be the last non-Black woman I would date so having a child was not ideal. I never believed in abortion. It did not sit well with me morally, and I saw the strain it had on the consciences of people I had known in the past. I did not want that. Taking a life for my recklessness. She also made it obvious that she wasn't going to have an abortion and having never had unwavering love in her life, I knew she needed something to love and someone who would love her, too.

I thought about the life of my future child often. More than likely, he would be fair skinned and able to choose to participate in Black culture or decide to "pass." I knew the results of Black men having children with White women. The color is drained. I saw this firsthand when I was in New Mexico. My uncle married a fair-skinned woman, which resulted in fair-skinned children. One of his sons procreated with White women, and there are hardly any traces of

Blackness within his children. So, if I could not keep my color, I would keep my name.

I knew there was no perfect way to parent. He would be his own person with his own personality. I would use guidance instead of control. I lucked out with a boy because the one thing I could be reassured of is the fact that every boy loves his dad. It is only after a series of disappointments does the heroic image fade in the eyes of the son. He would emulate me, and if he saw me doing the right thing, I would remain the hero in his eyes. I wanted to make sure he always saw me with a book but more importantly, I had to make sure I did nothing in the present that would tarnish my relationship with him in the future and always make him feel like he could come to me. Kids grow up and ask questions. I want to be able to tell my son I did the right thing.

My brother came out to visit me, and it's always nice seeing him. Tall, dark, muscular, and handsome. The women were always chasing after him. When I returned home for a wedding and popped up at a local bar where he and the other cousins were, he picked me up off the ground with joy, giving me the biggest hug.

A grown man, 5"11' 210 pounds, and he picked me up like a child. He saw a lot of the mistakes I made growing up and went down a different path. I've always felt more than fortunate to have him while growing up. There are certain memories you can only make with a sibling, and we had our share of them. Fighting with some neighborhood boys, unknowingly picking someone's roses for our mother, and almost burning down the house. He was big on reading, and when I started my literary journey, he would recommend books he thought I would enjoy.

At work, I kept seeing the vast contrast between myself and other non-Black employees. There was one employee, a White guy, who was not the best groomed. His beard was long and unkempt, yet he somehow managed to get a waitstaff position. At one event, he was scolded publicly by a manager for stealing bottles of liquor and was fired. I went to another event at a different catering company, and he was hired as the equipment manager. The catering community is small between full-time employees, so it was known that he had been fired for stealing. What really drove the point home for me was when I was walking through the city, and I thought I saw him on a bicycle. As he rode closer, I saw that it wasn't him but a homeless man. That's when I thought to myself "Wow, he got fired for stealing and got another job as a manager while looking like a homeless person." All because he's White, and he knew it. It made more sense when I heard him say to another coworker a few months ago when having a dilemma, "We're White, we'll make it work." It made me look at Whites differently and my sympathy for them faded away. I saw the confidence they carried because they knew that no matter how much trouble they were having or got into, the world would look out for them.

I was getting off the train one day in the city at Powell. As I was walking up the stairs to the street, a police officer was talking to a homeless man, telling him to move and he didn't want to see him there again or he would "jam him up," which is police talk for unnecessarily taking up your time. It let me know that what I was learning was true and useful. I got to the top of the street, and there was a brother standing there. He asked me, "Hey man! Who's your favorite author?" My guess is that he saw the book in my book bag. When I started to answer, he cut me off and said, "It's me," pulling out a book. Of course, I bought it and read it. I wanted to support any Black people I could. It was good. Even taught me some things about Korea. It had a few typos, but it was his, and he was proud of his work. That's when I realized that not everything is perfect and if this brother can do it, so can I. I ran into him a couple of months later and let him know how inspiring his work was.

I cherished my time with my Black coworkers. All of us sitting in a car, walking through the city, or huddled in a circle talking about the plight of Black people. All having similar stories. I said enough but not too much. After all, I was with a White woman, and I couldn't help but feel like a hypocrite. But I enjoyed sharing my knowledge and observing the reaction on peoples' faces when I knew something that they didn't. And that's what it is to be "different" as a Black person in today's society.

By now, I came to realize that everyone in America is biased. Or better yet, most of the world is programmed to see different cultures in a particular light. Stereotypes. The Latinos are hard workers and family-oriented. The Arabs are business owners and family-oriented. The Indians and the Chinese are intelligent. And the Whites? Well, they're the leaders. The heroes. All these cultures jump eagerly at the opportunity to fill the role assigned to them when society calls. This representation empowers them, and if you watch how they carry themselves, you'll see it. Anyone who constantly watches television is subject to this kind of thinking. Me not being the stereotypical Black male was what made me different. I had become the quiet slave.

I would see Dennis every now and then to grab drinks and see how he was adjusting to the single life. We would go out, and he would always offer to pay. I would tell him to stop and that you can't obtain genuine friends that way. The more you are willing to give, the more people are willing to take. I had also tweaked his online dating profile when he told me he wasn't having much luck. He said he got more "likes" after and was more receptive to what I had to say. By now, I was an expert at picking up women. I was constantly getting phone numbers, but I never called them. "The first thing to do is hit the gym. Women often want to feel secure with the man they are with. And just like you like looking at a nice body, so do they. Get some sexy underwear too. You like looking at them in sexy clothing? So do they. Leave a little bit of mystery. You always want a woman to feel like she's learning something new about you, so you must constantly be learning new things and unafraid to try new experiences. Women rarely cheat but when they do, it is often because they got bored with their partner. Always keep evolving your style and more importantly, remember this: no matter how fine she is, some guy somewhere is sick of her shit."

CHAPTER 11

We moved out of the apartment after our 18-month lease was up. They were going to up our rent and a lot of people were moving out. We moved a little further south to a town called Newark. It was a two-bedroom apartment next to a public library, park, and police station. It was also next to the train tracks. It wasn't the best area. You could see the belongings of other families lining the streets showing prior evictions. I vividly remember looking at the place and thinking to myself, "This is not going to end well."

By now my job had moved me to a wine bar under the Four Seasons hotel in downtown San Francisco. I enjoyed the spontaneity of catering, but decided to go with the wine bar for a consistent check. I was told by the chef at the time that when the kitchen manager left, I would be heir apparent.

I was able to learn a good bit about people's hidden biases while working there and the importance of being taken seriously as a Black man. There was a lot of down time during the job so while everyone else played on their phones, I read. And of course, everyone was surprised.

Shortly after I started, I had a disturbing encounter with one of the women in the office. I had been taking a side entrance through the valet area to avoid walking through the front of the wine bar. The valets were nice and asked where I worked, so I told them. They then emailed my job a picture of me, saying I wasn't allowed to enter there (I wondered why they didn't tell me themselves but soon realized that they were intimidated by me). That's when I met Waller, a White woman in her 40s who attended Harvard Business School. She rushed up to me asking about it, and when I started to respond she cut me off and told me I couldn't take that entrance. She was very rude. As she backed out the door to leave, I made sure she could see me roll my eyes. She returned a few minutes later (my guess was that she asked around about me) as I was kneeling in front of a cooler and stood there for a moment, waiting to be acknowledged. I made her wait until I got up. She introduced herself and attempted to make conversation, but I made sure to keep it short.

"So, you like to read, huh?"

"Yup."

"What genres?"

I studied her for a moment. I knew she genuinely didn't care. I saw her for what she really was, a dangerous woman of privilege. The only reason she was talking to me was because what she heard about me after she asked around was unexpected, and she was trying to save face. I decided to make her my project, and the results were more informative than I expected. I let everyone know I did not like her. Once word got around, she came into the kitchen and struck up a conversation about books with the chef, offering to buy him a copy of the book they discussed. I knew she was trying to bait me, but I didn't bite. I told upper management that she made me uncomfortable. I could see the effect it had on her. She was so used to being liked and catered to, the fact that she made someone uncomfortable (a Black man at that) was incomprehensible. In my eyes, she was the real threat. By now, White women calling police on people of color for no reason other than the fact that they didn't feel that they were being obeyed had been brought to light, and I saw her as that.

There were a few women (of different Latino

nationalities) who worked there and were very attractive. Once again, I fascinated them because I wasn't a "stereotypical Black." I was speaking to one of them, and she told me that she always saw Black men as players. "Have you ever dated a Black guy?" I asked.

"No."

"Then why do you see us as players if you've never dated one of us?" She shrugged her shoulders. Even though she didn't know why she saw us this way, I did – television and music. Entertainment had programmed her to think that we were all players that were up to no good and she didn't even know it. There was a pause during our conversation, and I knew exactly what she was thinking. She had been shown these inaccuracies and never had a desire to date a Black man, but I could see in her eyes I had changed that. There was dead air and I knew she was waiting for me to ask her out. As gorgeous as she was and as much as I wanted to, I had a baby at home. I could not, in good conscious, be out with a woman while Lexi was at home with the baby.

I enjoyed living near the library. I was

constantly checking out books. I picked up one on writing and started a journal. I would write short stories, skits, and letters to people as a therapeutic exercise. Lexi and I were watching a television show, and I commented how lackluster the scene was and that I could write a better one. It took a couple of days, but I did it. Shortly after, I thought about going back to school.

I tried college a couple of times when I was younger but didn't finish. I never knew what I wanted to go for. Now that I had a son, I had to look at my life and see the type of future I wanted and living paycheck to paycheck was not something I wanted for him. I decided the best thing to do was to try school again. I felt I needed some type of credential.

Lexi still wasn't working. She was able to get us some public grants and get us on WIC (which I later found out was inspired by the Black Panther Party of Self Defense), but it wasn't enough. She also had a credit card bill that would cripple us every month. We were in a tight spot and needed an exit strategy. A mutual friend of ours was in a similar situation saying, "Yeah, California is trying to kick us out, too."

My plan was to either ask my father to put me through school again or move back to North Carolina where I could work and go to school while we stayed at my mom's. That way, I could fast track and get my two-year degree. Lexi mentioned a third option: moving to a small town in Oregon. She had some relatives there and thought it would be a nice place to settle.

I had some paid family leave left over and decided to take the baby on a tour of the East Coast. A week in Ambler (outside of Philly) with my father's side of the family and a week back home.

My relationship with my father is no different than most sons who have a despondent relationship with their father. He was malicious and never understood the impact his words had on me. The words we speak to our children are essential to their growth. A child can feel the difference between tolerance and acceptance.

I went to visit him in my 20s and while we were in his backyard jacuzzi smoking cigars, he told me that if he could redo his life, he wouldn't have had children early. It was disheartening to hear because I was the only "early" child (he was 20 when I was born. My first sister showed up 9 years later). Ever since then, I've always felt like an extra in his family, and when I visited as a teen, there were subtle hints that were a precursor to this feeling. Although they were well-off and showered me with gifts, it always seemed disingenuous.

He and his family came out to see me shortly after my son was born. It had been a few years since we last saw each other. He didn't look too pleased when he wasn't named as a godparent. I knew he wanted the title of godparent for the novelty, not the duties that came along with it.

When they showed up, my stepmother brought me some Batman memorabilia. I had outgrown Batman some time ago, but she assumed that I was the same person I was in my early 20s. She hadn't grown, and she assumed I hadn't either. We were at Fisherman's Wharf when she got a peek into my bag. I was carrying some highlighters and a book. What did she do when she saw them? She threw her head back and laughed. She laughed at me for reading.

Before they left for the airport, my father pulled me aside and told me he was proud of me. I'd always wanted to hear those words from my father. When I finally did, they carried no weight.

I was excited to see family members I hadn't seen in years during this East Coast tour, more specifically, my grandfather. I had come to understand how fortunate I was to still have him and in my quest for knowledge of self, he could give me some of the answers I sought. Shortly after Thanksgiving dinner, I was able to sit with him and ask him questions about the family history. "The family name is Wolfe." He was born in 1936 and grew up in Atlantic City. The only child between his mother and father. He was born with the Wolfe name, which was his mother's maiden name. She ended up with another man whose last name was Collins and they had eight more children. When I asked him about his stepfather, he said, "All he taught me was how to smoke and drink."

"What about your father? Did you ever meet him?"

"Once. I was in my 20s. My mother told him that I was his son. He took one look at me and said 'No, he's not,' and walked out the door. I never saw him again. And I wonder how many kids he had.

Brothers and sisters, I don't even know."

"Why didn't you keep the Wolfe name? That's a pretty awesome last name!"

"Yea," he said with a chuckle. "Until the neighborhood kids would make fun of me. Always howling. So, I changed my name to my stepfather's." In fact, he rearranged his whole name, switching his first and middle name, too. After his mother passed, he spent most of his life searching for her birth certificate but never found it. I studied him closely as he revisited his past. Playing with a small piece of paper while staring blankly. My grandmother was at the table and commented on how the grandchildren were asking more about the family history.

I was with my father in his office when I saw my stepmother's brother's book. I came to realize that writing a book was not an easy feat. People don't watch movies or listen to music from 100 years ago, but they still read books from over 200 years ago. Books are ageless. "How was it?" I asked with enthusiasm.

"Eh, it was okay."

It's funny how a phrase or gesture can trigger a long-forgotten memory. I was about 11 or 12 when I went to visit my father one summer. He called my cousin and me up from the basement and out of nowhere started lecturing us. He asked us if we read. I told him I did and had a book with me, Shel Silverstein. When I showed it to him, he scolded me and said it was garbage. I stopped reading for years.

I was at a crossroad yet again in my life and because I knew he had the money, I asked him if he would be willing to put me through school. "Nah, it's too late for that." He could be crass, but he wasn't always wrong. It probably was too late, but I didn't feel like I had any other options. I was lost. He and my grandfather had been successful business owners at one time. Both starting from the ground up with no college degree. My grandfather made him create his own, and it was apparent he was going to continue the cycle. I hated asking him for money after he dropped us off at the airport.

During our visit he didn't change one diaper or offer to watch his grandson.

I thought about a lot on the plane ride from Philly to North Carolina. Connecting with a cousin about the frustration in trying to lift uplift our people.

Trying to give another cousin encouragement by telling him I saw parallels in our lives and reading would give him a sense of empowerment, but he just nodded and said nothing. Another cousin teaching me baby etiquette. One thing that stuck out to me was my grandfather saying, "Gee, parenting sure has changed since my day," after seeing me be so attentive to my son.

When we got to North Carolina I told my mom our situation and she agreed to let us stay with her. Two rules: no more babies and that Lexi do less helicopter parenting. I had talked with Lexi about giving our son a sibling. I value the relationship I have with my brother, and I wanted my son to have that. But more importantly, I didn't want him to be out in the world by himself after I was gone. This was another one of those cultural differences. Lexi did not like the guidelines and felt my mother was trying to have us under her thumb. To a Black person these were completely reasonable guidelines. In fact, these are universal guidelines in the Black community. I told her that she cannot have it both ways. We were in a tough spot and needed help. We left North Carolina with her upset with my mother, misinterpreting a lot of what was said.

The flight back to California was emotional. I knew Lexi and I were on borrowed time but her not getting along with my mother was a dealbreaker. My mother, like me, is very reasonable. Not only did she fly out to see Lexi in the hospital, but she also helped us get our first apartment and paid our rent when we were unable. She never mentioned it during tense conversations. My mother always stayed in my corner. During my time away from home I was able to see the relationship others had with their parents, and it made me realize how incredibly fortunate I am to have her as a mother.

When we returned home, we argued a lot. She would say harsh and hurtful things. She said things with no remorse. As Black people, we are taught to watch what we say because you cannot take back words. I pleaded with her, telling her that I felt this was the best option for us. But she didn't argue to understand, she argued to win. She said anything she could think of to try and hurt me. During one argument I told her I was done with our relationship.

She blew up, screaming and crying on the floor. I looked at our son as I held him as he watched his mother. That was when it dawned on me. This was her normal. Fighting, yelling, arguments. That is what she saw growing up. It wasn't normal for me, and I didn't want it to be normal for my son. I did not want him to equate abuse with love.

Work wasn't too much better. My reading made the front of house manager uncomfortable. The executive chef of the company had quit and shortly after, the chef at my location left. He was an Asian American named Jason. "They don't care about anything. They do what they want when they want to whoever they want with no remorse. They're shameless." Then he went home to his White girlfriend.

I inquired about the job, but they decided to go with a woman who didn't even want the job. Apparently, I did not suck up to the owner the way she liked. Saying "I just didn't feel a connection with him," which really meant that I didn't shuffle and dance to make her feel comfortable. I got a decent pay increase, but I had to train the new chef on how to do the job.

We still had to explore our third option, Klamath Falls, Oregon. I had never been that far northwest. Seeing the mountains in the distance reminded me of the Old Spice theme. I got to meet some of Lexi's family, who were nice enough. Her cousin threw a party one evening and had some of the locals over. I'm no stranger to being the only Black person at a party so I knew how to adapt. Only this time, I didn't want to. Everyone was nice, but something felt off. I couldn't put my finger on it.

There was one guy, I forget his name, but he did make to it a point to say, "I'm Black." When I raised an eyebrow, he went on further. "My father was in the military. He disobeyed orders so they sent him here. It's kinda weird. I have three siblings and we came out light, dark, light, dark." After we talked for a second, he went to talk to some other people. I looked him over and sure enough, if you looked closely, you could see the Black features. He was passing. I felt like I was looking at a possible future version of my son and it made me cringe.

I had never seen the stars more clearly than before that night. He followed me outside and told me more about the area. "If you go about five miles up the road, that's where the real hillbillies live. They'll shoot at your car as soon as you pull into their driveway." I got the sense that he was waiting for me to validate him as a Black man. Let him know that he was "down" and one of "us." "Yeah, not too many of us Black folks out here." He told me a story about when he worked on a fishing boat and if something didn't work, they called it the 'nigger' something. "I had to step in and say 'Whoa, my dad is Black, and that kind of talk is offensive' They actually got mad, so I had to find a job on a different boat."

It was at that party that I met what can only be described as the saddest woman in the world. She came into the party very quietly and everyone raced to greet her. "Her old man is a piece of shit," one of the guys told me. "He beats on her all the time." Generally, when someone says "all the time" you think maybe once a week or so. But in this case, it clearly meant every day, all day. She was quiet, and her face was permanently fixed in an expression that I can only compare to the tragedy theatre mask.

I got a glimpse of what my life would be like if

we moved to Oregon. If I were 10 years younger and still blissfully sleeping, I would've done it. But now that I was aware, I knew that by moving to Klamath Falls, I would be resigning myself to a life of isolation. There were very few Black people. And by a few, I mean two.

I went to the grocery store with Lexi's aunt where I saw a fair skinned Black woman in the parking lot. She made no eye contact. In the store, I stuck out like a sore thumb. I saw one other Black man working the produce section. I went and stood near him hoping he would look up and see he was not alone, but he never did. Almost like he had been by himself for so long he had stopped looking. I had come to understand how powerful my culture and color are and didn't want to fade away. I didn't want to become so accustomed to isolation that I don't look for my people.

We returned home in the same situation. Fighting, yelling, arguing. I was unhappy. Lexi agreed to move back to North Carolina then retracted. We were drowning, and she didn't want to leave. Unlike the last apartment (who were slightly forgiving when we fell behind on rent) this place started the paperwork immediately.

I read a book on how to spot deception. It specifically said, "Do not try this on your partner." But after some red flags popped up, I went through her phone and came across emails between her and the management company. When she first agreed to leave, I told her to let the management company know but instead, she tried to play the sympathy card. "I can't believe they would kick a family out on the street." I knew they didn't care. They wanted their money and now that she gave excuses instead of a plan, they were done. It was almost halfway through the month, and we did not have rent. Her credit card bill sunk us again, which forced me to do something I dreaded: call my father. It was always my family that saved us, and I resented her more for it.

Lexi eventually got a job working third shift as a hotel clerk. Her schedule synced with mine, so we didn't have to worry about babysitter. It looked like everything was going to be okay for a while. I was able to come up with a budget so we could make rent on time but when I called the management company, they didn't want to hear it. We fell behind one month and they evicted us along with two other families.

We ended up in Weed, staying on her family ranch while we tried to come to an agreement about the future of our family. I'd never stayed on a ranch before. It was nice. Calm and serene.

I still wasn't being cordial towards her mother. Shortly after we arrived, her mother pulled me to the side to talk to me. "I just wanted to apologize for saying that you were lying. I talked to him right after and he said that he did hit you first." I couldn't believe it. She knew I was telling the truth the whole time and after almost two years of me not letting her off the hook, she apologized. I could tell it was hard for her. That was when I learned that Whites are trained to not apologize to people of color.

The conversations between Lexi and me didn't get any better. I was still upset about the emails. It showed me how far she would go to have things her way. It made sense about that uneasy feeling I had in Oregon.

We got our tax return around that time, and I had to drive five hours back to East Bay to get it. I made sure to take my personal journal but left the journal for my son. When I returned, she mentioned something relating to a topic I spoke of in it. That's when I knew that I could not trust her. I told her I felt we were past the expiration date on our relationship and forcing something to work. There was enough money for us to each start over, but she didn't want to. After much debate she decided to move to North Carolina.

I knew that Lexi needed therapy and thought that if I could get it for her – we might have a chance. She sacrificed a lot for us, but her perception of a family was too warped for me.

The journey back home was arduous, and we spent most of our money to get back. We were back less than two weeks before things exploded. She was not accustomed to being in a calm home environment and a series of events one night brought the police to our door.

CHAPTER 12

I think about my journey out West often. The choices I've made and the consequences that followed. I understand how fortunate I was to have such a strong support system. People like my aunt and cousin. My mom's childhood friend, Shelly, who offered support and comfort during my mind splitting awakening. My good friend, Alan. Although I decided not to take him up on his offer for a place to stay (four people in a loft apartment would have been too much), he helped me with the set up of our baby shower and we always attended the Chinese New Year festivals together. High school friends who offered me a place to stay along my journey and the loved ones who came out and visited me.

I met some unforgettable people. Murph was a San Fransico native who I worked with in catering. He was always supportive and friendly. Irene, who helped me move when everything went down with Lexi's family. Rob, my barber that I started buying weed from once I realized that the major dispensaries were fixed to keep Black folks from being owners. My co-worker

Michael that I let sleep on my couch occasionally when I found out he was sleeping on buses at night. The boxer from Baltimore, Dwayne, who moved out west to escape gangs only to bring his wife who would drink and start fights with random people, resulting in him coming to work with bruises on occasion. The last time I saw Dwayne was on the BART. He was hanging with the meth heads.

I follow the lives of some through social media. I find it curious that some of the Black women I was around who sneered at me for being with a non-Black woman, didn't end up with a Black man. Jeni married a White man. Stephanie married a Filipino man and Marisa never married. I don't know what led to them make those choices. Maybe they felt they had no other options.

Although I felt I would have done some things differently, it had to happen the way it did for me to become the person I was meant to be. Everything I was waiting to experience back home was out there. I just had to conquer my fear of the unknown and go out and get it.

I would like to say my transition from "sleep"

to "woke" was gradual, but that would be a lie. It happened just like that. Tidbits of information; observing the words, personality, and actions of others; reading between the lines of media and entertainment; a sharper ear; a closer look at the world. And before you know it — that small tail led to a massive, manipulative, and dangerous snake. I had to learn that what was taught to me by society and entertainment was a lie. The lie being that we are all special. Unique. There are people in the world who are on our same path and who have been through the same experiences and felt the same pain. In this way, we are all connected, though we are made to believe we are not; taught to see each other as the enemy or competition.

Now, if you've made it this far – I thank you. I appreciate you, and I hope my story helps you during whatever personal journey you're on.

CONSCIOUS

Anytime I say something I know will be disturbing to some, I always try to word it the way I would like to receive it. Not in a diminished tone, but in an understanding tone. What I'm about to tell you will hopefully answer some of those inner questions we all ask ourselves. Like I said in the beginning, I'm going to touch on a few subjects that will make most people uncomfortable and some of y'all downright mad. But, before I do, I want to share my favorite quote.

"When at last Reason becomes the religion of men, then will the problem be solved."

-Adam Weishaupt

I want you to keep this quote in mind while you're reading this next section. You ready? That scene in the matrix when Neo wakes from his pod? OK, here it is.

Since the separation from my son's mother, I've been able to fully explore areas I was cautious of. Now that I have, I fully appreciate the restraint I used.

I believe that there are three main weapons that have been used to destroy Black people: religion, entertainment, and trauma.

Religion has been a very successful weapon against people of color. Before you get upset, let me ask, why is it that Black people are the only folks without a religion where our god looks like us? And what sense is it for a slave to have faith in the same god as his oppressor? And more importantly, what was the process to get the slave to accept his master's religion? Do you think our ancestors were asked nicely to accept a deity that doesn't look like them? Or do you think Black folks were beaten until they accepted it? I mean, the Ku Klux Klan called themselves "good Christians." (They were founded on December 24, 1865. That's right! Christmas Eve!)

During the colonization of our people, they (colonizers) cut off our ancestral roots and gave us the image of a White savior instead. They gave us a book (edited to omit any mention of uprising) telling us that it was "God's word" and if we follow these rules, we will be rewarded in the afterlife while they are rewarded in this life. These same people used this book to justify the genocide and enslavement of our people. A weapon to pacify us as they murdered, raped, and humiliated us while we prayed for mercy and salvation from their deity. They gave this same deity thanks after they finished murdering, raping, and humiliating us. Sitting around their dinner tables joyfully passing stories to their children and grandchildren about how we begged and prayed to their God before burning or hanging us. Christianity, Catholic, Baptist, Pentecostal, Mormon, Jehovah's Witness – none were created by Black people.

I found out through Dennis – a former Mormon - that in the Mormon religion, they are told that Black people are the descendants of Cain. For his defiance of God and betrayal of his brother, Abel, Cain and all his descendants were cursed with Black skin. My question is – what did Black people do to deserve this narrative? And, if this is told in the Mormon religion – what's told about Black people in other religions that we don't know about?

My aunt's Indian landlord was a complete jerk when I showed up. He tried to up her rent $700 to get me out. He was moving a couch one day, and my aunt (who's religious) asked me to go next door and see if he needed help. Why, though? Why should I help him when he's made it clear that he doesn't like my Black ass? I knew that if the roles were reversed, he wouldn't help me. If this man could, he would throw her out on the street and feel no remorse. I don't know his religion but if I could guess – whatever it is – it has nothing good to say about Black people.

In the 60s and 70s – when we controlled our own image – there was a genre of film called blaxploitation. These films gave us our own unapologetically Black heroes. Directors like Melvin Van Peebles and Gordon Parks showed us in a positive light, what we could accomplish, and how to defend ourselves from the racism we would face as Black people. They were eventually cancelled with the excuse being that the films caused a racial divide. I think the real excuse is because the powers that be wanted to control our image. It would be much easier to control the next generation if they saw themselves in a negative light.

I see the television for what it is - the great deceiver. There's a reason why old timers called it the 'idiot box'. Whites use the television to wash away their sins. The older generation of Black folk remembers though. They see it for what it is and know that the images we're given of Whites are inaccurate. It's my generation and younger who have been successfully fed lies and the White savior image.

"We are the only people on this entire planet who have been taught to sing and praise our demeanment. 'I'm a bitch. I'm a hoe. I'm a gangster. I'm a thug. I'm a dog.' If you can train people to demean and degrade themselves, you can oppress them forever. You can even program them to kill themselves and they won't even understand what happened."

-Dr. Frances Cress Welsing

Music was done the same way. What was groups of strong Black men and women singing about unity, family, self-knowledge, love, peace, etc., became music about disrespecting and harming one another. Only in Black culture do we have music that glorifies killing each other, disrespecting our women, and shunning education.

I no longer believe in celebrity worship. Now,

some of them are very talented and I do believe there are Black celebrities that do want to help the Black community. But they can only say so much. I mean, they do want to help, but not at the cost of their empire or lifestyle. And some of them will do or say things morally wrong (sometimes on the world stage) to maintain that lifestyle. What most people don't comprehend is that when you hit a certain tax bracket, you become accustomed to the numerous advantages that come along with it. I've noticed that it's the celebrities who've had everything taken away to be the legit ones. Craig Hodges, Muhammed Abdul-Rouf, Tommie Smith, John Carlos, Peter Norman, Muhammed Ali, Colin Kaepernick and many others. All of whom have been silenced or publicly humiliated and penalized for speaking the truth.

"Show me in the White community where a comedian is a White leader. Show me in the White community where a singer is a White leader or dancer, or trumpet player is a White leader. These aren't leaders. These are puppets and clowns that have been set up over the Black

community by the White community and have been made celebrities and usually say exactly what they know that the White man wants to hear."

-Malcolm X

And what of our Black leaders? The ones that could not be bought? They were either killed (some in front of their children) or jailed. Locked away so they cannot have an impact on the future generation until they are forgotten by society. Now, the justice system has righted some wrongs committed against 'us,' but it's always after repairing the damage is no longer an option. What good is it to exonerate someone 20 years after their death? Or after they've missed the opportunity for a full life with children and love? Society has mastered the art of giving Black folks VIP tickets to a concert that happened yesterday. And we fall for it every time.

"This country doesn't allow Black males to mature. It allows them to grow up physically but not to mature. Mentally, intellectually or spiritually. And Malcolm gave black men that

chance in this country."

-*Earl Grant (top aide to Malcolm X)*

****

"We must secure the existence of our people and a future for White children because the beauty of the White Aryan woman must not perish from this earth."

-*David Eden Lane (The Order)*

I was able to delve into the history of White culture and see how they've been able to stand strong for so long only by putting others down. How the history of slavery and the important role it played has been watered down. Keeping from us the fact that not only were slaves the victims of physical and mental abuse, but sexual abuse, too. This was done by White men and women. I put myself in the shoes of my ancestors and came to understand how powerful a weapon trauma has been on us.

Whites are programmed differently than other cultures. They aren't aware of it. Always used to being the center of attention. I can see why. During times of slavery and segregation, many Whites committed horrid atrocities (some were even paid to give interviews admitting to murder) then go home. Never facing any consequences. I'm positive they told their children, grandchildren, and great-grandchildren about their actions. How they were able to hunt us down and make clothes out of us. Passing down memorabilia from minstrel shows, lynchings, picnics, gator bait postcards, nigger hunting licenses, etcetera. How they bred us like animals and how we were seen as a commodity. How the Willie Lynch letters compared breaking slaves to breaking horses. How law enforcement was a tool created by Whites to wield with impunity against other races because deep down they know that they will always be looked at as the victim. I do believe there are good and sincere Whites, but there are far fewer conscious Whites. Only after continued observation and encounters will you be able to determine if they have achieved consciousness. These are not the ones who try to prove that they are "down." Quoting Black films, music, and books. I understand that Whites do have inquiries as to if they have hidden prejudices, but some go too far to prove their legitimateness.

While on YouTube a while ago, I saw an interview of White Fragility author Robin DiAngelo. She was being interviewed by journalist Michel Martin for the PBS show Amanpour and Company. The interview originally aired on Sept. 21, 2018. Here is the link: https://youtu.be/6O27_yBQ8Qc?si=vOA-PYSeaxlYj7o7.

The following is the transcript.

Michel Martin: *"What's 'White fragility? That's the title of your book, 'White Fragility,' and the subtitle is 'Why it's so hard for White people to talk about racism.' Why, White Fragility? And how do we recognize it?"*

Robin DiAngelo: *You know the 'fragility' part is meant to capture how little it takes to set White people off; to set us off into defensiveness. So, for many White people, the mere suggestion that 'White' has meaning will cause us to erupt in defensiveness. For many of your listeners, the fact that I'm generalizing right now about White people, will set off the defensiveness. Individualism is a really precious ideology for White people and we DO NOT like to be generalized about."*

MM: *So, let's back up a second and talk about how you got interested in this work and in this subject. I know that you're an* *academic. I know that you're a lecturer and also, you've done, what would you call it? 'Anti-racist training?'"*

RD: *"Yes."*

MM: *"It used to be called 'Diversity training.' Maybe that isn't called that anymore."*

RD: *"I think of myself as somebody who came from practice to theory rather than a lot of academics who go from theory to practice. So, I applied for a job in the early 90s for 'diversity trainer'. That's what we called it at the time. I thought, 'Of course I'm qualified to go into the workplace and lead people on discussions of race. I'm a vegetarian. How could I be racist?'*

"I had that really classic, liberal, open-minded kind of idea about what it meant to be racist and I saw myself, of course, as outside of that and felt qualified and I got the job. And I was in for the most profound learning of my life.

"It was a parallel process. So, two key pieces were: 1. For the first time in my life, I was working side by side with people of color who were challenging the way I saw the world. And part of being White is that I could get that far in life... I was a parent at that point, I was in my 30s and never had I had my racial worldview challenged -one; 2. Definitely not by a significant number of people of color and not in any kind of sustained way. And it worked like a mirror, right? I was like a fish being taken

out of water. I would not have been able to tell you I had a racial worldview because, as a White person, I was raised to see myself as just human. Now you're a particular kind of human; I'm just human. And if we're gonna be talking about race, I expect we're gonna be talking about your race, not my race."

MM: *"You tell some very interesting stories in this book. For example, you talk about leading a seminar where 38 out of the 40 people in the room were White, and then one of the participants literally pounds the table yelling, you know, 'White people can't get a job.' And everybody who had a job there was White."*

RD: *"It's a kind of delusion. I think that… I mean some people have said it, when you're used to 100 percent, 98 percent feels oppressive, right? As a White person, I was just raised to expect the world to be mine. In absolutely any field I see myself represented. I see myself represented in all my teachers and my curriculum and my heroes and heroines and so, just even the suggestion that we need to make sure we're being fair and including other people seems to set the White collective off."*

MM: *"Tell me some of the things that you saw in these workshops that led you to this theory."*

RD: *"It's a lot like water dripping on a rock, right? I didn't get it the first, second, third… but it's so consistent and so patterned* *that it's like a script, and after a while you can just stand there and say, 'I can predict what this White person is going say right now.' And sure enough, they say it. 'I was taught to treat everyone the same'; 'I have people of color in my family'; 'I was in Teach for America'; 'I marched in the 60s'; 'I taught in a diverse school.'*

"The evidence that White people give for their lack of racism is very revealing to what we think racism is. And everything I do is to try to get us off the surface - which is all these narratives - and get under there to the underlying framework. Because despite all those narratives, 'I was taught to treat everyone the same', 'I don't see color', our outcomes haven't improved. By virtually every measure, there is racial inequality in this country; and by many measures, it's increasing not decreasing."

MM: *"You speak very frankly in the book about how you've stepped in it yourself…if I can use that phrase. Can you give an example of where you experienced your own White fragility?"*

RD: "So, I'm in a room with three Black women. Two of which I'm very close to and one I don't know at all. And she gives us a survey to fill out and it's tedious to me. It seems kind of template. It doesn't capture the nuance of what we do. So, I push it aside and I say, 'Let me explain…we go out into these different offices and we do these anti-racism trainings. In fact, Deborah here was asked not to come back when she went to such-and-such office…I guess her hair scared the White people.' She has long locked braids.

"So, I want you to notice what I'm doing. Not only am I making a joke about a Black woman's hair, which is a sensitive issue and I do know better, but I'm positioning myself as the 'cool' White person and they're all the clueless White people.

"And I wish I could tell you that I recognized I was doing that. I didn't. Meetings over. Couple days later the assistant, Marsha, comes to me and says, 'Angela was really offended by that joke you made about Black women's hair.'

"And I immediately…., 'Oh God, thank you!' And I called Angela and I said, 'Would you be willing to grant me the opportunity to repair the racism that I perpetrated towards you in the meeting last week?' She said yes.

"We sat down we talked about it and she said, 'I don't know you. I have no relationship with you. I have no trust with you. And I do not want to be joking about Black women's hair in a professional work meeting with a White woman that I don't know.'

"'I hear you. I apologize.' Then I asked, 'Is there anything I missed?'

"And she said, 'Yes. That survey you so glibly shoved aside…I wrote that survey. And I have spent my life justifying my intelligence to White people.'

"Own that. Apologized. Asked, 'Is there anything else that needs to be said or heard that we might move forward?'

"And she said, 'Yeah. If we're gonna work together, I'm sure you're gonna run your racism at me again. And so, the next time you do, would you like your feedback publicly or privately?'"

MM: "Interesting…"

RD: "Haha! Well, I love her for that. I said, 'Publicly, in my case, please.' It's really important that other White people see that I am not free of this. But it gives me an opportunity to model non-defensiveness."

MM: "You said you don't want White people to feel guilty, which is exactly what I think some people listening to our conversation will feel and will think that you want to evoke. So why do you say you don't want White people to feel guilty?"

RD: "Well, because you didn't choose your socialization. You didn't choose your conditioning. You were born into a society that set you up in these ways. You don't need to feel guilty unless you know that and you're not doing anything about it."

MM: "What about…"

RD: *"Go ahead."*

MM: *"The people who voted for Obama and then voted for Trump?"*

RD: *"I think that Obama was symbolic. I think what Obama did was allow us to feel really good about ourselves under very narrow terms, right? If the word racism ever came out of his mouth, I don't know what would've happen, right? He had to be the perfect Black man, right? The safe Black man.*

"He's also brilliant, and clear, and educated. And also at the same time, that allows me to feel good about myself.

"There's also a little bit of challenge there in how powerful a Black man he is. And I would ask any White person who voted for Obama and sees that as kind of their evidence that they're free of racism to ask themselves, 'How did it change your life on the ground? How did Obama's presidency change the lived experience for Black people in this country, day-in and day-out?'

"I don't think that it did. It was important symbolically, but mass incarceration, school-to-prison pipeline… these things have not diminished, right? In many ways, they've increased."

MM: *"Do you see Trump as a reaction to Obama? And if so, why?"*

RD: *"I see Trump as a reaction to Obama because Trump gave permission to the resentment that was roiling under the surface."*

***MM:** "Resentment of what?"*

***RD:** "Of Black advancement. Of Black uppity-ness. To use a Jim Crow analogy, 'You will step off the curb when I come down it. You will not look me in the eye.'*

His racism is explicit and undeniable. And that wasn't a deterrent. I think White people have to look really hard at why was that not a deterrent to you."

***MM:** "Robin DiAngelo, thank you for talking with us."*

If they really want to know – all they must be is their true selves and we (Blacks) will let them know if they have racist and prejudice tendencies, but they must be willing to accept the truth they're being told.

"Being friendly and being a friend, I think, are two different things. I think there are many Whites who act friendly towards Negroes. A fox acts friendly towards the lamb and usually, the fox is the one who ends up with the lamb chop on his plate. The wolf doesn't act friendly and therefore the wolf has more difficulty in getting the lamb chop on his plate. I say that because if you study the structure of the Negro community,

economically, politically, civically, psychologically and otherwise - it's controlled by the White liberal who usually poses as a friend of the Negro who actually differs from the White conservative in the same way that the fox differs from the wolf. Their appetite is the same. Their motives are the same. It's only their mannerisms and methods that differ."

-Malcolm X

And that truth is, everything in America is rooted in racism.

****

"It's been a long, a long time coming but I know, a change gonna come, oh yea it will."

-Sam Cooke

No, it's not! That song came out in 1964 and ain't shit changed. If it did change – I wouldn't be writing this book. And do you know what happened to Sam Cooke? He was killed. Not only was he killed. His

145

dead body was photographed and put on national display. I've never seen a White celebrity's dead body displayed. But change is gonna come, right? Black people today are subject to the same treatment as the 1960s. Don't believe me? Ask your elders or pick up a book.

****

I know it wasn't easy digesting what I've just told you. But hey…I did warn you. Now, I'm sure after everything I've told you, you feel hopeless. "You just told me everything I know and have been raised to believe is a lie." You're probably thinking, "You just told me religion, celebrities, entertainment, politics, and society is bullshit and la dee da. What do I believe in, then?" Nigga! Believe in us. When you fully comprehend the steps taken to hold us back – you'll see how powerful WE truly are.

I look at the state of my people, and it pains me. Angry and confused. Taught only to lash out at each other with no understanding of why. Unable to see that society has created these conditions for us. If only they would pick up a book and see what empires and civilizations our people have created, they would begin to wake up, have a stronger sense of pride, and see that we are all one.

"I do believe there will come a time when the Black man will think like a Black man and he will feel for other Black people and this new thinking and feeling will cause Black people to stick together. Then, at that point, you'll have a situation where when you attack one Black man, you are attacking all Black men and this type of Black thinking will cause all Black people to stick together. And this type of thinking also will bring an end to the brutality inflicted upon Black people by White people, and it is the only thing that will bring an end to it. No federal court, state court or city court will bring an end to it. It is something that the Black man has to bring an end to, himself."

-Malcolm X

There was a time when I thought that was never gonna happen. Or, if it did, it would be too late. But if it does happen, the first step is for niggas to pick up a book.

✳✳✳✳✳✳✳✳✳✳✳✳

I have a few unorthodox solutions. Before I present them – you must understand that this system was never designed for us. I came across the solutions because, out of everything we've tried, these seem to be the most effective. Why? Anytime there is Black love or massive and organized unity amongst our people, the establishment snuffs it out. Deacons of Defense, Congress of Racial Equality (C.O.R.E), the M.O.V.E organization, the Black Panther Party of Self Defense (not to be confused with the Black Panther Party of Northern California. Bobby Seale called them "paper panthers." Cultural nationalists who were "jive" and would show up to protest with no bullets in their guns). They were effective. They were only created to combat social injustice; mistreatment by the justice system and corrupt police when the system turns a blind eye. They gave us a sense of pride. Feeding the community through social programs, educating us on our history and how to navigate and combat the system using knowledge. Why are these organizations labeled as "militant" and "radical," but the Ku Klux Klan is still operational?

Politics? That was never designed with us in mind. We've all seen it; the politician who comes to the neighborhood kissing babies and giving speeches. Making promises and claiming to have your best interests at heart, only to be unavailable once they've secured your vote. Politics is just the delaying of a decision until it's no longer relevant. I mean, it's called the right and left "wing" because they are part of the same "bird" – so to speak. I have seen some candidates who seemed hopeful, but they can only do so much before they have to "play ball" or be removed from the game. And if you get out of line, the thin blue line will knock you right back in line.

The cognitive dissonance is thick and no matter how much you try to gain understanding and sympathy, they don't care. It's gotten to the point where even when you're defending yourself, you can still be portrayed as the aggressor. So, these are my solutions. None will be easy.

One solution would be Polygamy. Why? Between false incarceration and unjust killing – the numbers are skewered when it comes to the ratio of

Black men to Black women. Discovering that Black men were the only ones subjected to the "man out of the house" rule made me understand how powerful Black male presence is. We also must remember that the marital laws we follow were created by a religion that was/is used as a tool to divide and oppress us. Before organized religion, Africans and Indigenous Americans practiced polygamy. Not in the perverted way it has been twisted by society but as a more stable family unit. It's much easier to dismantle a family with one husband and wife than it is with one husband with two or three wives. This leaves the family in-tact should one choose to leave or be taken away by some misfortune. Everything the establishment gives us is only to further their own agenda, and if you look at it as a military strategy, it makes perfect sense to enforce monogamy on a population you need to keep under your boot heel. A numbers game if you will. But more importantly, I believe that polygamy will give roots to our future generations. A child who knows their heritage and ancestors.

But will this happen? I don't think it will. We are too ingrained with the oppressors' religions. The campaign for Black women to see each other as competition has been successful, and Black men are not in the right mindset to take on such a task.

I often think about how polygamy could have helped in marital situations. Husbands and wives left alone in their grief while shouldering whatever family duties that must continue. Someone to help with the raising of children or help with the coping of the loss of children. Someone to mediate disagreements and misunderstandings between persons. A broader financial base, which would lay a more solid foundation for the future generation. I believe this can also create a sisterhood that seems to have been lost among Black women. For this to successfully take place, there must be raw transparency and each partner must have true knowledge of self and always strive for the status of godhead.

Another solution? Our own territory. A place where we can truly feel safe and create for ourselves free from bigotry, racism, and systemic oppression. Will this happen? Again, no. Why? I've asked myself that question a few times. After all, every other nationality has a place to call "home." Other nationalities born in the United States can go to their "home" country and feel welcomed. Even the Jews got Israel after the Holocaust in 1948.

After slavery, Blacks were released by Whites (with no compensation while slave owners were monetarily compensated for each slave they released) with the belief that we would not be able to make it on our own but, they were proven wrong. Our ancestors pulled themselves up from nothing to create towns, run successful businesses, create schools and institutions, and put our own style on sports. We did this so well in fact, that Whites carried out coordinated attacks on us (e.g. Red summer of 1919) throughout the country. Why? I honestly believe - that Whites believe - if they were to give us our own territory, we would eventually take back this planet that is rightfully ours. So, integration was forced. To keep an eye on us and ensure we don't reach our full potential.

This would also show White Americans that it is their own government picking their pockets.

The establishment is slowly erasing past transgressions against Blacks. Soon there will be a society of youth who have no knowledge of what transpired in the past. The fact that our own established towns and neighborhoods were violently taken away from us with no compensation. Our own territory would undo the actions of their ancestors. This would also help ease the consciences of Whites who see that something is wrong but do not know what to do. Not to mention the ones that don't want us here.

Last option? Boycotting. We used to boycott. Now we protest. The difference? Protests make noise, but boycotting disrupts the money flow.

Most people are familiar with Rosa Parks and the Montgomery Bus Boycott. You know, Black people had to sit in the back of the bus until Rosa Parks refused, and the result was the integration of buses. (Fun fact: Claudette Colvin was pre-Rosa Parks, but she didn't have the right "image.") Because...Blacks in the area boycotted. It didn't take a week or a month, it took over a year. December 5, 1955 – December 20, 1956. That means for over a year, we had to walk and carpool before we were offered equality. A year! We had to hit them pockets! That takes a lot of discipline. Something we as a people have lost. And they know we don't have the discipline. That's why they keep doing it.

"Give them bread and circus and they will never revolt."

-Juvenal (Roman poet)

We'll keep watching the game, following trends, and buying into traditional holidays never meant for us. Funding a system that has shown repeatedly that they do not care or value us outside of what we can do for them.

****

I now fully comprehend how I and my people are perceived by society. And the truth is – I'm just a nigger. That is until I open my mouth and prove otherwise. No one cares for the words of a Black man outside of entertainment. Every time a Black man opens his mouth to educate, there is always someone with a rebuttal. Eager to prove him wrong. Not arguing to understand, but to win.

My perception of the world has transformed, giving me the cursed foresight to see how bleak the future is for mankind. We are living in an orchestrated apocalypse. What the majority of the population fails to understand is that we are pampered as a society. We don't have to think. We are told what to eat, where to shop, who to love and hate, who to worship, and what music to listen to.

We are under constant surveillance and coerced by a system that is willing to adapt to complete the conquest for a new world order. Anyone deemed a true threat will be slandered in the media, discredited, or killed. How do I know? It's right there in the history books.

There will be no mass awakening or global revolution. This is a fantasy given to us by television. The same entity that glorifies trauma, violence, revenge, love, and conquest. This is what gives us unrealistic expectations and causes us to be constantly disappointed by the world. People must also understand that celebrities and politicians will not give us the tools to liberate ourselves. Their goals will always be money and power.

****

So, I guess we should address the obvious

question. You're probably asking yourself – how this nigga talking all this pro-Black shit and got a mixed kid?

"And she want love, you only want sex. You got yours, she didn't get hers. She got no respect, y'all had a son. She like "fuck you" she only wanna check. The little nigga gonna lose."

-Lupe Fiasco (NGL)

It wasn't any easy choice. I understand that I have gambled with erasure. If my son decides to be a part of White culture (b/c it's easier) that's the risk I took. But I ask you this – what was I supposed to do? Abandon him? Feed into the stereotype that Black men abandon their children? I mean, I still am a Black father. I reflect on the separation from his mother and the effect it might have on him. But for me to become the best father I can be, I would have to be happy. I felt it was better for Lexi and myself to be happy separated rather than miserable together. If we stayed together, who knows what crutches I would use to numb the pain of an unhappy relationship, and I didn't want my son to have memories of an onery father.

The only thing I can do is prove to my son that what White culture says about Black men is wrong. So, when he's with his White friends and they speak negatively, he can say "Hold up! My father is Black. That's not true." My only hope is that since he'll be straddling the line, he'll get a front row seat to how each culture thinks. He'll know firsthand what is being said behind closed doors. Then, he can choose for himself which culture he wants to partake in. If he does choose White culture – there's nothing I can do. It isn't about me. And, as a parent, I want what's best for him. That's just the reality of it.

I know he will start to ask questions when the kids at school call him a half breed and such. And, I'll have to tell him the truth – he was born under less-than-ideal circumstances, but I don't love him any less. I'll have to apologize for the position I put him in. I've placed him in the middle of two cultures that are polar opposites. Anytime he's felt uncomfortable or isolated – it's all my fault. But I will be a constant in his life. His true north.

I've come up with every justifiable (or so I thought) answer for dating outside my culture. The truth of the matter is, you cannot be pro-Black if you do not have a Black spouse or Black offspring. And, what of the ones who speak pro-Black but choose to marry and procreate with non-Blacks. It is only when in their 70s and 80s, when they are looking at a family picture of their children and grandchildren and great grandchildren will they think to themselves – if I love being Black so much, why am I the only nigga in the picture? I understand why you did it – you felt no appreciation from those in your culture but at what cost?

Why is something that was taboo and illegal at one point, something that Black men were killed over, now pushed in front of us? What's the endgame? What is the price of constant discomfort? Raging inner conflict? What is the price of feeling constant and underlying judgement?

Every time there's an event that rocks my culture – my spouse couldn't relate. Sympathize but not relate. Akin to seeing a documentary about a culture thousands of miles away. You see it and sympathize, but it doesn't rock you to the bone. And now that you have clearly been shown the difference –

you feel stuck. How do you tell someone that you love everything about them but their culture? Especially when children are involved. The answer? Well, every situation is different. But when you start to hear those drums in the distance calling you home…they never go away.

The only justification would be to clearly say — that's what I like. Which is fine. Just understand that you have no voice when it comes to Black issues.

The truth is — non-Black spouses are easier to deal with. But have you ever asked yourself why? Well, I'll tell you. The reason it's easier to get along with non-Black spouses is because they haven't been through what we have. I can guarantee that although these other races have had their trials and tribulations, one thing that keeps them reassured is the fact that they glad they ain't Black. Why? They know that Black people all over the world are subject to harsher treatment than anyone else. The saying "As bad as things are — at least I'm not a nigger." Sound ridiculous? Let me ask you this — have you ever asked your non-Black spouse what they've heard about Black people growing up? It might surprise you.

So, now if you're thinking – ok, I gotcha but what am I supposed to do? Just leave? Well, that depends on how much mental stability means to you.

I understand the fear and hesitation, but know there is a place for you here. It won't be easy. It will be the hardest thing you'll do. The ticket "back home" does not come cheap. You just have to ask yourself if you're willing to pay the price.

It will take painful self-healing and unity. We all must ask ourselves – what are we willing to sacrifice for freedom and equality? Only we can heal us. Only we can save us. More importantly, only we can keep our culture strong.

****

In a society where everyone can give their opinion, very few people listen to real knowledge. Why? Because it shatters the veil placed in front of our eyes that tells us everything is alright if it doesn't directly affect us or our loved ones. If people were able to "wake up," they would see the helpless situation we are in as a society and that there is no fighting or changing the system. It has grown too large and too powerful. Operating per design while making you think you have a fighting chance.

The only way to win is to not participate. But how many are willing to make that sacrifice? To give up the comforts of the lives we live to build our own shelters, stitch our own clothing, and hunt and grow our own food. The world would adjust, but mass chaos would ensue as the strong eat the weak. This is something society is not ready for. Only when we decide to unite as a collective by showing that we can survive without the system, will change begin to take place.

www.ingramcontent.com/pod-product-compliance
Lightning Source LLC
Chambersburg PA
CBHW050915260726
48660CB00001B/217